# Contents

| | |
|---|---|
| Unit: Growth and Changes in Plants | 2 |
| Unit: Forces and Movement | 24 |
| Unit: Stability and Structures | 44 |
| Unit: Soil and the Environment | 65 |
| STEM-Related Occupations | 89 |
| Early Engineers: The Wright Brothers | 90 |
| Early Engineers: Alexander Graham Bell | 92 |
| Early Inventions:Telephones from the Past | 94 |
| New Inventions: The Clean Water Book | 97 |
| Amazing Robots | 99 |
| When I Grow Up... | 102 |
| Engineering in Our Daily Lives | 103 |
| Engineers Make Our Lives Better | 104 |
| Think Like an Engineer! | 105 |
| The Design Process | 106 |
| STEM Vocabulary | 110 |
| How Am I Doing? | 111 |
| STEM Rubric | 112 |
| STEM Focus | 113 |
| Achievement Awards | 114 |
| Answer Key | 115 |

As we live in a rapidly changing society, exposure to and fluency in Science, Technology, Engineering, and Mathematics (STEM) ensures students will gain the skills they will need to succeed in the 21st century. It is essential that students gain practice in becoming good problem solvers, critical thinkers, innovators, inventors, and risk takers.

# Teacher Tips

## Encourage Topic Interest

Help students develop an understanding and appreciation of different STEM concepts by providing an area in the classroom to display topic-related non-fiction books, pictures, collections, and artifacts as a springboard for learning.

## What I Think I Know / What I Would Like to Know Activity

Introduce each STEM unit by asking students what they think they know about the topic, and what they would like to know about the topic. Complete this activity as a whole-group brainstorming session, in cooperative small groups, or independently. Once students have had a chance to complete the questions, combine the information to create a class chart for display. Throughout the study, periodically update students' progress in accomplishing their goal of what they want to know, and validate what they think they know.

## Vocabulary List

Keep track of new and content-related vocabulary on chart paper for students' reference. Encourage students to add words to the list. Classify the word list into the categories of nouns, verbs, and adjectives. In addition, have students create their own science dictionaries as part of their learning logs.

## Learning Logs

Keeping a learning log is an effective way for students to organize thoughts and ideas about the STEM concepts presented and examined. Students' learning logs also provide insight on what follow-up activities are needed to review and to clarify concepts learned.

Learning logs can include the following types of entries:

- Teacher prompts
- Students' personal reflections
- Questions that arise
- Connections discovered
- Labeled diagrams and pictures
- Definitions for new vocabulary

# What Do Plants Need?

Here are things that plants need to stay alive.

**Air:** Plants need air just like you need air. You take in air through your nose and mouth. The leaves and roots of a plant can take in air.

**Water:** All types of plants need water. Plants that grow outdoors get water from rain. Indoor plants need to be watered. Outdoor gardens need to be watered when there is not enough rain.

**Light:** Plants use sunlight for energy. Some plants need more sunlight than others. Some plants can grow in shady places. Other plants need a lot of bright sunlight.

**Warmth:** All plants need warmth. Plants in a garden do not grow in winter because it is too cold. Some plants grow well in very hot places, such as deserts. Other plants grow well in places that are warm, but not too hot.

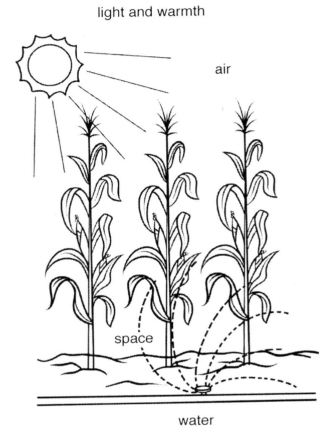

light and warmth

air

space

water

**Space:** A plant needs enough space to grow. A plant's roots need space to spread out in the soil. If too many plants are growing close together, they may not get enough sunlight, water, or nutrients.

On many farms, fields are planted in rows. The space between each row gives each plant enough space for its roots to spread out. The plants are not too close together, so each plant can get enough light.

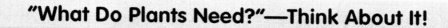

# "What Do Plants Need?"—Think About It!

1. Some of the things plants need are things that people need, too. In the chart below, write an "X" to show things that plants need and things that people need. The first one is done for you.

| | Plants | People |
|---|---|---|
| Water | X | X |
| Time to sleep | | |
| Air | | |
| Soil | | |
| Warmth | | |

2. Why do many indoor plants grow well near a window?

_____

_____

_____

3. A large plant will not grow well in a small pot. Explain why.

_____

_____

_____

_____

4. Name a type of plant that you like. Tell why you like it.

_____

_____

_____

_____

# Parts of a Plant

Read the chart to find out about the different parts of a plant.

| Part of a Plant | What Does This Part Do? |
|---|---|
| Roots | The roots grow in soil and soak up nutrients and water for the plant. Roots also hold the plant in place, so the wind does not blow it away. |
| Stem | The stem carries nutrients and water from the roots to the rest of the plant. The stem also holds up the plant. |
| Leaf | Leaves make food for the plant. Sunlight gives the leaves energy to make food. |
| Flower | Flowers grow fruit and seeds so that new plants can grow. Seeds are usually inside the fruit. You can see tiny seeds on the outside of strawberries. |

## Think About It!

**1.** Label the parts of the plant.

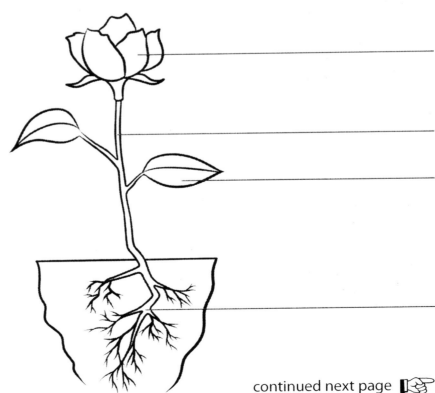

continued next page

Answer the plant riddles.

**2.** Food and water move through me from the roots to the rest of the plant.

What part of a plant am I? _____

**3.** You cannot see me because I grow underground.

What part of a plant am I? _____

**4.** Because of me, a plant grows seeds.

What part of a plant am I? _____

**5.** We are two parts of a plant. Without us, plants would not have food.

What parts of a plant are we? _____ and _____

**6.** I am the part of a plant that grows fruit.

What part of a plant am I? _____

**7.** On a tree, I am very tall. On a dandelion, I am short.

What part of a plant am I? _____

**8.** I am the most colorful part of many plants.

What part of a plant am I? _____

# Parts of a Flower

What do the different parts of a flower do?

**Sepals:** A flower starts out as a flower bud. On the outside of the flower bud are small green leaves called sepals. The sepals protect the flower growing inside. When the flower blooms, you can see the sepals at the bottom of the flower.

**Petals:** Some flowers have large petals, and some have small petals. The petals are often brightly colored. The petals can make birds and insects want to come to the flower.

**Pistil:** The pistil is in the middle of the flower. At the bottom of the pistil is a thick part where seeds grow.

**Stamens:** The stamens are long and thin. They grow all around the pistil. The top part of the stamen makes a powder called pollen. Pollen from the stamen gets on the top of the pistil. Then a seed grows in the pistil.

continued next page 👉

## Making Seeds

A flower makes seeds. Pollen helps make the seeds. Pollen must get from the stamen to the pistil. How does this happen? Wind can blow pollen from the stamens to the pistil. Or, insects can move the pollen. An insect might visit the flower and land on a stamen. Some pollen sticks to the insect's feet and body. That pollen can rub onto the pistil when the insect passes it. Pollination happens when pollen gets on the top part of the pistil.

### Think About It!

**1.** How many of each part does a flower have? Circle the correct answer.

| | | |
|---|---|---|
| **Petal** | one | more than one |
| **Sepal** | one | more than one |
| **Stamen** | one | more than one |
| **Pistil** | one | more than one |

**2.** Fill in the blanks.

Flowers have a powder called _____. The powder is on top of a

_____ . A flower can make _____

when the powder gets to the top of the _____ .

**3.** Brightly colored petals can make insects want to come to the flower.
How do insects help flowers?

_____

_____

_____

_____

_____

# Life Cycle of a Plant

Read about the life cycle of a plant that makes fruit with seeds inside.

1. A seed gets water. A tiny plant pushes out of the seed.

2. A root begins to grow down into the soil. The stem grows up out of the soil. Now the plant is called a sprout.

3. The sprout's stem grows taller and leaves appear. Now the plant is called a seedling.

4. Over time, the plant grows larger. More leaves grow. The plant becomes an adult plant. Now it can grow flowers.

5. Each flower turns into a fruit that has seeds inside. The fruit falls on the ground and rots away. The seeds do not rot. The seeds get buried in the soil and the cycle starts over.

**Seed Facts**

A seed always grows into the same type of plant that made it. A seed from an orange only grows into an orange tree.

One plant can make many seeds. Why do plants make so many seeds?
Some of the seeds might not grow into adult plants. Here are two reasons why:
• The seed might fall on rocky ground where it cannot grow.
• The seed might fall in a dry place. It might not have enough water to grow.

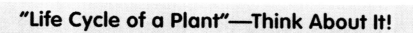

**1.** Label the life cycle diagram. Use the words below.

   **adult plant**      **seedling**      **seed**      **sprout**      **plant with fruit**

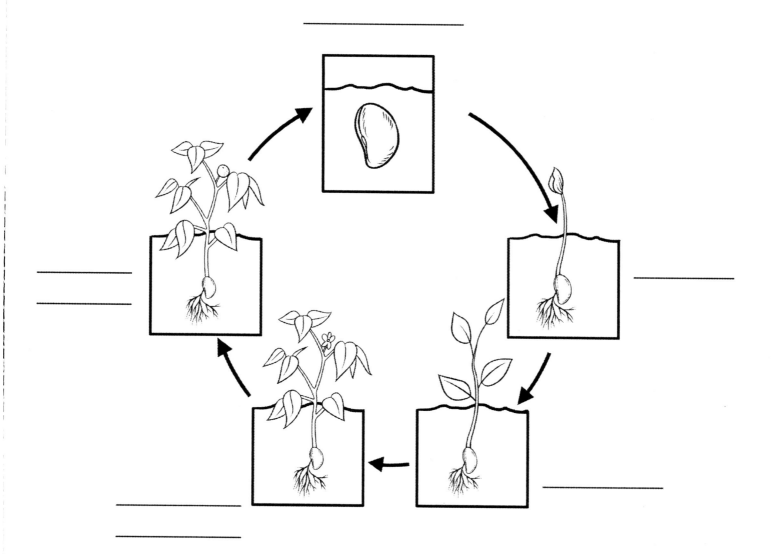

**2.** Tell a partner about the life cycle of a plant. Explain how it makes fruit with seeds inside. Use the diagram to help you.

# Experiment: Watching Seeds Grow

How long does it take seeds to start to grow? Try this experiment to find out.

## What You Need

- A clear plastic cup
- 1 dry kidney bean
- 1 dry chickpea
- Water
- Potting soil
- Ruler
- Masking tape

## What You Do

1. Soak the kidney bean and chickpea in water overnight.

2. Fill the cup half way with soil.

3. Put the kidney bean on top of the soil. Push it against the side of the cup.

4. Put the chickpea on top of the soil. Push it against the other side of the cup.

5. Add more soil to the cup. Leave about 1 in. (2.5 cm) between the soil and the top of the cup.

6. Use masking tape to label the seeds. Put the labels near the top of the cup, where there is no dirt.

7. Pour a little water on the soil. Do not water too much!

8. Put the cup in a warm, sunny spot. Water the soil a little every day.

9. Look at the seeds every day. Record what you see.

## "Experiment: Watching Seeds Grow"—Think About It!

### Predict

1. How many days will it take for the kidney bean to start to grow roots? _____

2. How many days will it take for the chickpea to start to grow roots? _____

3. How many days will it take for the kidney bean to become a sprout?

   (When the stem grows out of the soil.) _____

4. How many days will it take for the chickpea to become a sprout? _____

### Think

5. You put the cup in warm, sunny spot. Why is that important?

   _____

   _____

   _____

   _____

   _____

   _____

6. Kidney beans and chickpeas are seeds that people eat. What other seeds do people eat? Name at least four.

   _____

   _____

   _____

   _____

   _____

# "Experiment: Watching Seeds Grow"—Observations

Draw and write about what you see. Remember to check your predictions.

| Date: | |
|---|---|
| Kidney bean drawing | Chickpea drawing |
| **Notes:** | |

| Date: | |
|---|---|
| Kidney bean drawing | Chickpea drawing |
| **Notes:** | |

**Energy**

All living things need energy. Plants need energy to grow larger and to grow flowers and fruit. People and animals need energy to grow and to move.

# How Do Plants, Animals, and People Get Energy?

Plants get energy from the Sun. They use the energy in sunlight to make food for themselves. The food gives the plant energy to grow.

People and animals cannot get energy from sunlight. Plants contain energy from the Sun. People and animals can eat plants to get energy.

Many people and some animals get energy from eating meat. Meat comes from animals. For example, people eat beef which comes from cows. Cows contain energy they got from eating plants such as grass. The grass got energy from sunlight. All of this energy started out as the energy in sunlight.

**Energy from the Sun goes into grass.**　　**Energy from the grass goes into the cow.**　　**Energy from the cow goes into a person eating beef.**

A hawk eats snakes. Snakes do not eat plants, but they do eat small animals that eat plants. Look at how the energy that starts as sunlight gets to the hawk.

**sunlight　➔　plants　➔　small animal　➔　snake　➔　hawk**

# "How Do Plants, Animals, and People Get Energy?"—Think About It!

**1.** All food contains energy. Where does the energy come from first?

_____

_____

_____

**2.** What do plants use energy to do?

_____

_____

_____

**3.** What are two things that people use energy to do?

_____

_____

_____

**4.** How does energy from the Sun get into a cow?

_____

_____

_____

**5.** Fruits and vegetables come from plants. Fruits and vegetables contain energy that the plants got from sunlight. List four fruits and four vegetables that people eat.

| Fruits | Vegetables |
|--------|------------|
|        |            |
|        |            |
|        |            |
|        |            |

# Seeds On the Move

Imagine if all seeds sprouted close together. Soon the plants would be crowded. Each plant would not have enough water, light, and space to grow well. Seeds can travel away from the parent plant that made them. Traveling helps seeds. The seed may land in a good place to grow.

## How Do Animals Help Seeds Travel?

Here are a few ways that animals help seeds travel:

**Manure:** Animals eat fruit that contains seeds. The seeds take time to move through the animal's body. The seeds come out in the animal's droppings (called manure). The manure may end up far away from the plant that made the fruit.

**Hiding Places:** Some animals hide fruits and nuts (a type of seed) so they can eat them later. For example, a squirrel finds a nut. The squirrel carries the nut to a different place and buries it. The nut might grow into a plant if the squirrel does not come back.

**Hooks and Spikes:** Some fruit or seeds are covered in hooks or spikes. One example is called a burr. You may have seen burrs stuck to your pants or shoes. The hooks or spikes on the burr get caught in an animal's fur. Then the seed is carried on the animal until it falls off. The seeds may fall off far away from the plant that made them.

burr

# "Seeds On the Move"—Think About It!

**1.** Each dandelion seed is attached to a bit of white fluff. How does wind help a dandelion seed travel?

**dandelion seed**

_____

_____

_____

_____

**2.** Maple seeds have a wing cover. Sometimes two wings with seeds are attached to each other. The seeds spin as they slowly fall to the ground. How can wind help maple seeds travel?

_____

_____

_____

_____

**maple seed**

**3.** How do people help seeds travel to different places?

_____

_____

_____

_____

_____

_____

# Helping Each Other

Here are some ways that plants and animals help each other.

> Plants provide food that gives animals energy. Animals eat food, then leave manure on the ground. Manure is a fertilizer that helps plants grow.

> Plants grow fruits that animals eat. These fruits contain seeds. The seeds come out in the animal's manure. The animals leave manure in different places. This helps seeds travel to different places.

> Animals need oxygen, which is in air. Animals take in oxygen when they breathe. Animals breathe out carbon dioxide. This goes into the air.

> Plants need the carbon dioxide that animals breathe out. Plants use the carbon dioxide to make their own food and release oxygen into the air.

**Plants Help People**

Plants help people, too. Here are a few examples:

- People get energy from the plants they eat. People also eat animals that eat plants.
- People need to breathe in the oxygen that plants make.
- People make useful things from plants. Cotton is a plant used to make clothes. Many medicines come from plants. Trees provide wood for paper and to build furniture and houses.

## "Helping Each Other"—Think About It!

Complete the sentences. Fill in the blanks with one of these words:

**animals**          **people**          **plants**

**1.** Birds build nests from sticks and twigs.

This is an example of how _____ help _____.

**2.** Trees provide shade that helps keep houses cool in summer.

This is an example of how _____ help _____.

**3.** Bushes provide insects with a place to hide.

This is an example of how _____ help _____.

**4.** People water and fertilize their gardens.

This is an example of how _____ help _____.

**5.** Rope can be used in many different ways. Rope can be made from plants.

This is an example of how _____ help _____.

**6.** Insects visit flowers. This helps pollen get from the stamens to the top of the pistil. This makes plants produce seeds.

This is an example of how _____ help _____.

**7.** Sometimes plants are growing too close together. Animals eat some of those plants. The plants that are left can grow better.

This is an example of how _____ help _____.

# Growing Plants for Food

Read about four places where people grow plants for food.

## Farms

Farms have large fields where plants grow. Many farms grow corn, wheat, and oats. Wheat is used to make bread. Many breakfast cereals contain oats. Corn is used in food and other products.

## Orchards

Most types of fruit grow on trees. An orchard is a tree farm. Many orchards in the United States grow apple trees and peach trees. Some orchards grow trees or bushes that produce nuts. Walnuts grow on trees. Peanuts grow in the ground under a bushy plant.

## Greenhouses

Greenhouses are buildings with roofs and walls made of glass. All that glass lets in sunlight. Plants growing inside get a lot of light. Sunlight also provides plants with the warmth they need to grow.

Greenhouses are warm inside. This makes it possible to grow plants in colder weather. Tomatoes, cucumbers, peppers, and lettuce are some of the foods that grow in greenhouses.

## Home Gardens

Many people grow food in a home garden. They might grow carrots, tomatoes, lettuce, and green beans. Food from a home garden is fresher than food from a grocery store. Growing your own vegetables is fun!

# "Growing Plants for Food"—Think About It!

**1.** Trees in an orchard are planted far apart from each other. You can see this when the trees are very young. Why is it important to plant trees far apart?

_____

_____

_____

_____

**2.** How do greenhouses help us have vegetables during winter?

_____

_____

_____

_____

**3.** Why is food from a home garden fresher than food from a grocery store?

_____

_____

_____

_____

**4.** What are your favorite foods that come from plants?

_____

_____

_____

_____

# Plant Parts: I Ate That?

People eat lots of plants, but do you know which *part* of the plant you are eating? It might surprise you to know that celery is a stem. For each food, name the plant *part* we eat.

**stem     flower     seed     bulb     leaf     root     fruit**

cauliflower _____

onions _____

lettuce _____

pear _____

melon _____

beet _____

peas _____

lemon _____

zucchini _____

corn _____

carrot _____

eggplant _____

asparagus _____

apple _____

What plants do you like to eat? _____

_____

# Create a Board Game About Plants

## What You Need

- Scissors
- Glue
- 2 number cubes
- Construction paper
- Coloring materials
- A base for the game board, such as poster board, a clean pizza box, or a file folder

## What You Do

1. On the board game base, draw a path that the game pieces will follow. Some path ideas are: a U shape, an L shape, a square, or an oval. Make your path at least 50 squares long.
2. Add spaces where you have to stack question cards. Print instructions on some game board spaces.
3. Make question cards by printing or writing questions on heavy paper.
4. Test the game to see if it is too difficult or has enough spaces.
5. Cut small figures out of paper to use as game pieces, or use materials that are available such as bottle tops, candy, or small toys.
6. Decorate the game board to make it colorful so people know it is about plants.
7. Write the rules and directions on how to play the game.

## Rules and How to Play

- How does a player move around the board? Here are some ideas:
  - roll the number cubes
  - pick up a card and answer a question
  - follow the instructions on the game board spaces
- Are there penalties for wrong answers?
- How many players can play?

## Ideas for Game Cards

Create questions about plants to test players' knowledge. Create different categories such as:

- true or false
- explain
- multiple choice

## Ideas for Game Board Spaces

- miss a turn
- go back 5 spaces
- roll the number cubes again

# Plants Quiz

Use the clues to fill in the blanks.

**1.** Three things on a flowering plant. All begin with **S**.

_____     _____     _____

**2.** Two parts of a flower that begin with **P**.

_____     _____

**3.** Two names for a young plant starting to grow. Both begin with **S**.

_____     _____

**4.** Something animals make that helps seeds travel. The word begins with **M**.

_____

**5.** Two things that begin with **O**. One is something people need to breathe. The other is a place where many trees grow.

_____     _____

**6.** Two things that plants need to stay alive. Both begin with **W**.

_____     _____

**7.** Two things that grow on many plants. Both begin with **F**.

_____     _____

**8.** Plants get this from the Sun. People and animals can get this from eating plants. The word begins with **E**.

_____

**9.** Two places where people grow plants for food. Both begin with **G**.

_____     _____

# What Can Forces Do?

## Forces Make Things Move

A soccer ball sits on a field. The ball will not move by itself. Can you make the ball move? You could kick it.

You want to get socks from a drawer. How do you open the drawer? You pull the handle.

Objects need a force to make them move. You kick a soccer ball with your foot. You pull a drawer with your hand. Pushing and pulling are forces. Forces make things move.

You use *muscular force* to push and pull.

## Forces Make Things Stop

Forces can also make objects stop. A shopping cart will roll down a hill. You can stop the cart by grabbing the handle. Or you could push against the cart. Pushing and pulling are forces. Pushing and pulling can make objects stop moving.

## What Else Can Forces Do?

**Change speed:** Forces can change the speed of an object. You push a toy car to make the car start moving. To make the car go faster, you can push the car harder. You can use force to change the speed of a moving object. The second push makes the car go faster.

**Change direction:** Forces can make an object change direction. To change the direction of a baseball that is pitched to you, you hit the ball with a bat. When you hit the baseball, you push the ball with the bat. The baseball changes direction and moves away from you.

## "What Can Forces Do?"—Think About It!

Which type of force do you use for each action below? Write **push** or **pull** beside each action.

**1.** Pick an apple from a tree. _____

**2.** Ring a doorbell. _____

**3.** Throw a ball. _____

**4.** Undo a zipper. _____

## Read this story:

Tanya put her dog Sparky on a leash and took him for a walk. Sparky started to run down the sidewalk. This made Tanya run. Tanya got tired of running. She used the leash to make Sparky slow down. Then Sparky saw a squirrel and began to chase it. Sparky pulled Tanya right through Mr. Lee's flower garden!

**5.** What are the pulling forces in this story? Give two examples.

_____

_____

**6.** Force can change the speed of something. Give two examples from the story.

_____

_____

**7.** A pulling force changes the direction of a moving thing. Give an example from the story.

_____

_____

# The Force of Gravity

Gravity is the force that makes things fall. Gravity is a force that pulls things to the ground. Gravity stops objects from floating up. Gravity holds things down.

Remember four things that forces can do:

1. Make an object start moving
2. Make an object stop moving
3. Change the speed of an object
4. Change the direction of a moving object

The force of gravity can do the same things.

## Gravity Makes an Object Start Moving

If you let go of a ball, the ball drops to the ground. You do not need to push the ball to make the ball fall. Gravity makes the ball start moving.

## Gravity Makes an Object Stop Moving

If you toss a ball up, the ball will soon start to fall. Before the ball starts to fall, the ball will stop in the air. The ball stops for a very short time. You do not see the ball stop. The force of gravity makes the ball stop going up.

## Gravity Changes the Speed of a Moving Object

When an object falls, the object moves faster and faster as it gets closer to the ground. Gravity makes things move faster as they get closer to Earth.

## Gravity Changes the Direction of a Moving Object

If you throw a ball to a friend far away, the ball starts to fall. The direction of the ball changes. The ball starts to fall down. Gravity changes the direction of the ball.

## "The Force of Gravity"—Think About It!

**1.** Why does gravity make you go down a slide?

_____

_____

**2.** When you go down a slide, do you move faster near the top of the slide or near the bottom? Tell how you know.

_____

_____

_____

_____

_____

**3.** In space, there is little gravity. What do you think happens if you pour juice into a glass in space?

_____

_____

_____

_____

_____

**4.** Think about riding a bicycle. How does gravity help you move?

_____

_____

_____

_____

# The Force of Magnets

A magnetic force is the push or pull action of a magnet. This force can move objects without touching them.

## What Do Magnets Push?

Magnets can repel, or push away, other magnets. Magnets have two ends. One end of the magnet is called the north pole. The other end of the magnet is called the south pole.

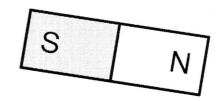

The north pole of one magnet will push away the north pole of another magnet. The south pole of one magnet will push away the south pole of another magnet. So two north poles of two magnets repel each other. Two south poles also repel each other.

## What Do Magnets Pull?

Magnets can also attract, or pull, on each other. Opposite poles on magnets attract each other. The north pole of one magnet will attract the south pole of another magnet.

There are many types of metals. Some metals are magnetic and some are not. Iron and nickel are two types of metals that are magnetic. A magnet has a pulling force on iron and nickel. Magnets are attracted to those metals.

## Why Do Magnets Stick to Some Metals?

A magnet keeps pulling on a metal object. The magnet pulls even when it is touching the object. That is why a magnet does not fall off a refrigerator door. The pulling force of the magnet keeps the magnet stuck to the door.

# "The Force of Magnets"—Think About It!

Look at each pair of magnets. **N** shows the north pole of each magnet. **S** shows the south pole of each magnet. Write whether the magnets will pull together or push apart.

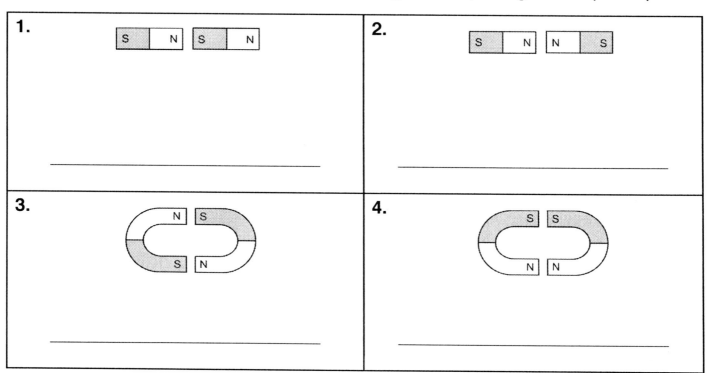

Pablo rolled a small iron ball near a magnet.
The dotted line shows where the ball rolled.

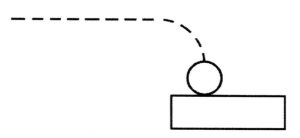

5. What does Pablo's experiment show? Put a check mark beside each correct answer.
   (There may be more than one correct answer.)

   ❏ Magnetic force can make an object start moving.

   ❏ Magnetic force can make an object stop moving.

   ❏ Magnetic force can change the direction of a moving object.

# The Force of Friction

## What Is Friction?

Friction is a force. Friction is created when things rub against each other. What does friction do? Friction slows objects down.

Imagine you push a box across a smooth floor. The box moves, then stops. The box and the floor rub against each other. There is friction between the floor and the box. Friction works against movement. Friction makes moving objects slow down.

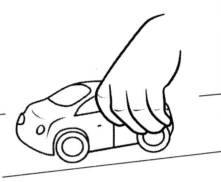

smooth surface

## Smooth and Rough Surfaces

When objects rub against each other, their surfaces touch. Rough surfaces create more friction than smooth surfaces.

Imagine pushing a toy car across a hard floor. Now imagine pushing the car on carpet. The car slows down on both floors, then stops. On which floor will the car go farther? Why? The carpet has a rougher surface than a hard floor has. The carpet creates more friction. When there is more friction, an object slows down more quickly.

rough surface

## Surfaces Rubbing Together

What happens when different surfaces rub against each other? Does the amount of friction change?

| What Rubs Together? | How Much Friction? |
|---|---|
| A rough surface rubs on a rough surface | A lot of friction |
| A rough surface rubs on a smooth surface | Medium friction |
| A smooth surface rubs on a smooth surface | Very little friction |

## "The Force of Friction"—Think About It!

Use the examples below to answer questions 1 and 2.

• You roll a marble on a towel.

• You roll a marble on a glass table.

**1.** In which example is more friction created?

_____

_____

_____

_____

**2.** Tell why you think your answer to question 1 is correct.

_____

_____

_____

_____

**3.** Imagine you rub together two pieces of regular paper. Then you rub two pieces of sandpaper. When is there more friction? Tell how you know.

_____

_____

_____

_____

**4.** Cars go faster on a paved road than on a gravel road. How can friction explain this?

_____

_____

_____

_____

# How Friction Helps Us

How does friction help us in daily life? Friction stops us from slipping.

## Slippery Ice

There can be lots of ice on sidewalks in winter. Ice is very smooth, so ice is easy to slip and hurt yourself on. Why? A smooth surface rubbing against a smooth surface creates very little friction.

**winter boots**

Winter boots help us from slipping on ice. Why? A rough surface rubbing against a smooth surface creates medium friction. Winter boots have rough soles that create friction. Friction slows or stops movement. Thus, the rough soles on boots stop us from slipping on ice.

Sometimes people put sand on ice. Sand makes the ice surface rough. It is harder to slip on sandy ice. The sand creates friction between the ice and your boots.

## Slippery Stairs

**wood stairs**

Slipping on stairs is very dangerous. You could hurt yourself badly if you fall down the stairs.

Stairs are often made of smooth wood. When shoes rub against smooth wood, there might not be enough friction. The shoes might slip off the step. Socks are even worse.

Carpet can add friction to stairs. Rough strips of material work, too. The added friction stops people from slipping.

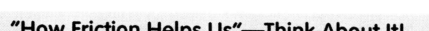

## "How Friction Helps Us"—Think About It!

1. Think about going down stairs wearing socks on your feet. Now think about going down stairs wearing athletic shoes. Which example is more dangerous? Tell why.

_____

_____

_____

_____

2. In winter, some cars have snow tires. Snow tires help people drive in snow. Snow tires also help cars stop faster.

   In summer, cars have regular tires. Which tires have a rougher surface: snow tires or regular tires? Why do you think so?

_____

_____

_____

_____

3. People do not leave snow tires on cars all year. When spring comes, people put regular tires back on.

   Why do people not leave snow tires on all year?
   (Hint: Think about friction and what it does.)

_____

_____

_____

_____

# A Snowy Day

As you read the following story, think about the types of forces in it.

It was Saturday morning. Kim sat at the kitchen table.
She ate breakfast with her mom and her little brother, Ryan.

Mom poured milk on Ryan's cereal. "We are almost out of
milk," Mom said. "Kim, would you please write *milk* on the
shopping list?"

Kim pulled the shopping list from under the magnet on the fridge door.
She wrote *milk*, then put the list back under the magnet. Mom asked,
"Kim, did you look outside?"

Kim looked out the window. Big, fat snowflakes were falling from the sky. She pulled the
drapes open wider. "It is snowing!" shouted Kim. "It is the first snowy day of winter."

Kim jumped up and slid on the tile floor in her sock feet. She pretended she was skating.
"I want to go skating," she said.

Ryan tried to slide on the floor, too. "I cannot slide," he said.

"Ryan, you are wearing running shoes," said Kim. "Running shoes have rough soles.
You cannot slide in running shoes."

Ryan looked sad. "I want to slide, too!" he said.

Mom said, "I will take you both tobogganing today. Then you can slide down hills."

Kim and Ryan shouted, "Hurray! We are going tobogganing!"

Mom picked up Ryan and put him back in his chair. She pushed his bowl of cereal
toward him. "We should hurry and finish our breakfast," said Mom. "I want to go
tobogganing, too!"

## "A Snowy Day"—Think About It!

Complete the chart. Name the force for each example from the story.

**muscular force     magnetic force     gravity     friction**

| Force | Example from the Story |
|-------|------------------------|
| 1. | Sliding down hills on a toboggan. |
| 2. | Kim pulls the drapes open. |
| 3. | Ryan cannot slide on the floor in running shoes. |
| 4. | A magnet makes the shopping list stick to the fridge door. |

Find more examples of forces in the story.
Do not use examples from the chart above.

5. Gravity: _____

_____

6. Gravity: _____

_____

7. Muscular force: _____

_____

8. Muscular force: _____

_____

# Contact and Non-contact Forces

## What Is Contact?

When two things touch each other, we say they are in contact with each other. When your hand touches a book, it contacts the book.

## Contact Forces

Some forces work through contact. You use muscular force to push and pull objects. To push a toy car across a table, you need to contact the toy car. Muscular force is a contact force. To push or pull an object with your muscles, you need to have contact with the object.

Friction is another contact force. Friction happens when two objects rub together. The two objects must be in contact with each other. If there is no contact between the objects, there is no friction.

## Non-contact Forces

Some forces can work without contact. If you hold a magnet near a pin, the pin will move toward the magnet. Magnetic force makes the pin move, but the magnet is not touching the pin. There is no contact. Magnetic force can work even when there is no contact between objects.

Forces that can work without contact are called non-contact forces. These forces can work when there is distance between the objects.

Gravity is another non-contact force. Gravity pulls objects toward Earth. Snowflakes fall to the ground because gravity pulls them down.

## "Contact and Non-contact Forces"—Think About It!

**1.** Write the forces below in the correct column of the chart.

**friction**      **magnetic force**      **muscular force**      **gravity**

| Contact Forces | Non-contact Forces |
|---|---|
|  |  |

Use the pictures to help you answer question 2.

**Magnetic force makes a nail stay in contact with a magnet.**

**The force of gravity keeps a rock from floating in the air.**

**2.** Do non-contact forces work *only* when there is no contact between objects? Give reasons for your answer.

_____

_____

_____

_____

_____

_____

_____

_____

# Experiment: The Force of Static Electricity

Have you ever felt a shock after walking across carpet? That shock comes from static electricity. Try this experiment to see what static electricity can do.

## What You Need

- A sink
- A plastic comb
- Medium or long hair

## What You Do

1. Comb the hair at least ten times.
2. Slowly bring the comb close to a thin stream of water. (Do not let the comb touch the water.) Watch what happens to the water.
3. Finish the pictures below to show what you saw. Draw the stream of water.

**What the stream of water looked like before the comb got close to it**

**What the stream of water looked like when the comb got close to it**

## "Experiment: The Force of Static Electricity"—Think About It!

**1.** In this experiment, does static electricity create a pulling force or a pushing force? Tell how you know.

_____

_____

_____

_____

**2.** Is static electricity a contact force or a non-contact force? Tell how you know.

_____

_____

_____

_____

**3.** Would the same thing happen to the water if you used a magnet instead of a comb? Tell why or why not.

_____

_____

_____

_____

_____

**Try It!**

Cut a small piece of tin foil into 6–8 very tiny pieces. Comb your hair at least ten times. Bring the comb close to the tin foil pieces, but do not touch them with the comb. What happened?

# Wind and Water

When wind and water move quickly, they have a strong pushing force. What can this pushing force do?

## Wind

Wind is air that is moving. Wind creates a pushing force. Have you been outside on a very windy day? Strong wind can push you so hard that you almost fall over.

Hurricanes are storms with very strong winds. Hurricane winds can knock over trees and break windows. They can even blow the roof off a house.

Tornadoes are storms with wind that moves in circles. A tornado makes a shape like a funnel. It is wide at the top and narrow at the bottom. Tornado winds have very strong force. Some tornadoes are so strong that they blow down houses. They can even flip cars and knock over heavy trucks.

## Water

When water moves quickly, it has a strong pushing force. A flash flood is a flood that happens quickly. The water moves fast over land and causes a lot of damage. A flash flood can push cars. It can even push a house off its basement foundation. The flood can also carry away soil that plants need to grow.

The pushing force of wind creates waves. Strong wind creates large waves that can be very dangerous. Large waves can wreck boats or houses on the shore. Very large waves can cause a flash flood.

## "Wind and Water"—Think About It!

1. Even gentle wind has pushing force. List three things you have seen that show the pushing force of wind.

_____

_____

_____

_____

2. A basement may be a good place to go when there is a tornado. Why would being upstairs be more dangerous?

_____

_____

_____

_____

3. Why would a basement *not* be a good place to go if a flash flood is coming?

_____

_____

_____

_____

4. How can the pushing force of wind create a flood?

_____

_____

_____

_____

# Mix and Match Forces Game

1. Cut out the cards on this page and mix them up.
2. Take a card. Place the card on the square it goes with on the next page. Place only one card on each square.
3. Continue until you have placed all the cards.

| | | |
|---|---|---|
| Examples of muscular force | They make things start moving, stop moving, change speed, or change direction | Gravity |
| Magnets have two of these | Push apart | A force that happens when two things rub together |
| Two non-contact forces | Two contact forces | This force makes a ball fall to the ground when you throw it |
| These create friction so we do not slip | Something created by the pushing force of wind | A safer place in a house during a tornado |
| You create this when you comb your hair | What a magnet attracts | A storm with wind that moves in circles |

continued next page ☞

# Mix and Match Forces Game Board

| | | |
|---|---|---|
| The basement | Friction | What the north poles on two magnets do to each other |
| Rough soles on shoes | Pushes and pulls you create with your body | A wave |
| Gravity | Objects made of the metals nickel or iron | Gravity and magnetic force |
| Static electricity | The pulling force that comes from Earth | Tornado |
| Friction and muscular force | Poles | Things forces can do |

# What Is a Structure?

skyscraper

A *structure* is something that holds or supports a load. A truck can hold a heavy load of boxes. A *load* is something that has weight.

Your bed is a structure that supports a load. When you lie on your bed, you are the load. The bed supports the weight of your body.

## A Structure Has Size

Structures come in many different sizes. A skyscraper is a huge structure. A skyscraper supports the weight of all the people, furniture, and equipment inside it.

A paper cup is smaller than a skyscraper, but a paper cup is a structure, too. When you fill a paper cup with water, the water is the load. The cup has to support the weight of the water.

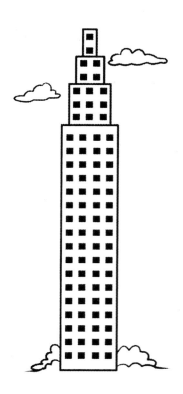

skyscraper

## A Structure Has Shape

A structure can be almost any shape. A bookcase is a structure shaped like a rectangle. Buildings are structures. Think of all the different shapes that buildings can be. An airplane and a helicopter are both structures that can fly. They each have a different shape.

airplane            helicopter

## A Structure Has a Purpose

A structure is built to do something. A bed gives you a soft place to lie down and sleep. A bookcase stores books. A truck carries large, heavy loads from place to place.

# "What Is a Structure?"—Think About It!

**1.** What do all structures do?

_____

_____

**2.** The load a structure supports can be made up of more than one thing. For example, people, furniture, and equipment are all part of the load in a skyscraper. Name two things that might be part of the load in each structure below.

An airplane: _____    _____

A backpack: _____    _____

A shopping cart: _____    _____

**3.** What load is a skateboard made to hold? What is the purpose of a skateboard?

Load: _____

Purpose: _____

_____

**4.** Is a fence a structure? Use the information from the text and your own ideas to explain your thinking.

_____

_____

_____

_____

_____

_____

_____

# Natural Structures

You can find many structures in nature.
Look at the two examples below.

## Trees

A tree is a structure. A tree holds a load, has size and shape, and has a purpose.

It is easy to see that every tree has a size and shape. What load does a tree hold? A tree has to hold up the weight of its trunk, branches, and leaves. If a tree cannot hold up this load, it will fall over.

What is the purpose of a tree? A tree makes seeds so other trees just like it can grow.

## Beehives

Bees make a home called a beehive. Thousands of bees can live in one beehive. Bees make honey, and they store the honey inside the beehive.

A beehive is a structure. A beehive has size and shape. The load that a beehive holds includes the bees and the honey. The purpose of a beehive is to give the bees a home, a place to store food, and a place to keep their eggs safe.

tree

**Beehives often hang from tree branches.**

**Brain Stretch**

Make a list of other structures found in nature. _____

_____

_____

_____

_____

## "Natural Structures"—Think About It!

1. Many birds build homes called nests. Name two different things that can be part of the load in a bird's nest.

   _____        _____

2. What is the shape of a bird's nest?

   _____

3. What are some materials a bird uses to build a nest?

   _____

   _____

4. Spiders build structures called webs. What is one purpose of a spider web?

   _____

   _____

5. What are two things that can be part of the load on a spider web?

   _____

   _____

6. Beekeepers raise bees and sell the honey the bees make. A beekeeper builds special beehives where the bees live. Is this special type of beehive a natural structure? Tell why or why not.

   _____

   _____

   _____

   _____

   _____

   _____

# Strength and Stability

## Strength

A structure has to be strong enough to hold its load. A chair is a structure. The person who sits on the chair is the load. If the chair is not strong enough, the chair will break when someone sits on it.

A paper cup does not have to be nearly as strong as a building. The liquid in a paper cup does not weigh very much.

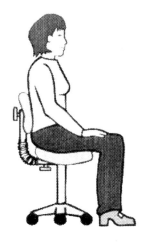

A person who sits on the chair is the load.

## Stability

We say that a structure is stable when the structure can keep its balance and stay in place.

It is easy to keep your balance when you stand on two feet. Standing on two feet keeps you stable. Keeping your balance when you stand on one foot is harder. When you stand on one foot, you are not as stable. You might sway back and forth, so your body does not stay in place.

Have you ever tried to create a very tall stack of nickels? When the stack is short (less than 25 nickels), it is stable. The stack does not sway or jiggle much when you add nickels. Once the stack has about 40 nickels, it jiggles and sways much more. A short stack of nickels is more stable than a tall stack of nickels.

Have you ever tried to create a very tall stack of nickels?

## Challenge

How long can you stand on one foot? Have a contest with your classmates.

## "Strength and Stability"—Think About It!

Tanya's mom built a simple step to help her reach things on high shelves. She nailed a thin piece of wood on top of two thick blocks of wood. Then she stood on the step.

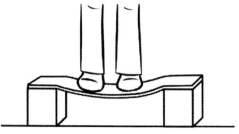

1. Does the step look strong? How do you know?

_____

_____

_____

_____

2. Does the step look stable? Explain your answer.

_____

_____

_____

_____

3. What could Tanya's mom do to make the step stronger?

_____

_____

_____

_____

4. Why would it be important for a step like this to be stable?

_____

_____

_____

_____

# Choosing Materials

When people build structures, they need to choose the materials that will work best in the structure. Here are some things people think about when choosing materials.

**Strength:** A structure must be strong enough to hold its load. To build a strong structure, you need to use materials that are strong. Shape adds strength, too.

**Flexibility:** A flexible material can bend without breaking. Most diving boards are made of flexible materials. One end of the diving board bends down when the diver jumps on it. Then the diving board goes back to the shape it was in, and this pushes the diver up in the air.

**Durability:** A durable material is one that will last a long time. A building made of stone blocks will last much longer than a building made of wood. Stone is a more durable material than wood.

People also think about how easy it is to shape the material. Wet concrete and clay can be shaped by pouring them into a mold. Steel can be melted and poured into a mold. Wood can easily be cut into different shapes. Machines can cut stone into blocks. Making other shapes from stone is more difficult.

# "Choosing Materials"—Think About It!

**1.** Glass is a material used to make windows. What are two reasons to use glass?

_____

_____

_____

_____

**2.** Some ancient stone buildings are still standing more than 1,000 years after they were built. What two properties does this tell you stone has?

Stone is a _____ building material.

Tell how you know.

_____

_____

Stone is a _____ building material.

Tell how you know.

_____

_____

**3.** A shoe is a structure. Shoes hold a load. (You are the load.) They have a size and a shape, and they have a purpose. (They protect your feet and keep them comfortable.) Explain why it is important to use a flexible material to make shoes.

_____

_____

_____

_____

_____

# Experiment: Make a Paper Bridge

How strong can you make a paper bridge?

## What You Need

- 50 nickels (or more)
- Notebook paper
- Books
- Ruler

## What You Do

1. Make two stacks of books. Each stack should be the same height.
   The stacks should be at least 2 in. (5 cm) tall and about 6 in. (15 cm) apart.
2. Place the sheet of paper flat across the two stacks to make a bridge.
3. Put nickels on top of the paper one at a time. Count how many nickels you can add before the bridge collapses. Record your results on the next page.

4. Fold the paper in half as shown.

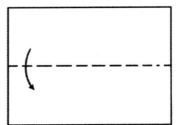

5. Fold the paper in half again, as shown.
   Repeat steps 2 and 3.

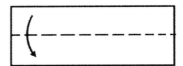

6. Unfold the paper and fold it again as if you were making a paper fan.
   Repeat steps 2 and 3.

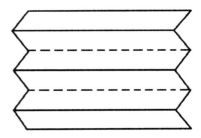

## "Experiment: Make a Paper Bridge"—Observations

## Observations

Use the chart below to record your observations.

| Step | How the bridge was made | How many nickels did the bridge hold without collapsing? |
|------|------------------------|----------------------------------------------------------|
| 3 | | |
| 4 | | |
| 5 | | |
| 6 | | |

## Think About It!

**1.** Which of the paper bridges was strongest? Tell why you think it was strongest.

_____

_____

_____

_____

_____

_____

**2.** How could you build a strong bridge with two pieces of paper? Think of different ideas and test them. On another piece of paper, make a chart to record your observations.

# Experiment: Center of Gravity

Every object has a spot that is called the center of gravity.
Try this experiment to find the center of gravity of a ruler.

## What You Need

- 12 in. (30 cm) ruler
- Eraser
- Masking tape
- Partner

## What You Do

1. Balance the ruler on your finger. (Move your finger right or left to find the spot where the ruler balances.) This spot is the ruler's center of gravity.

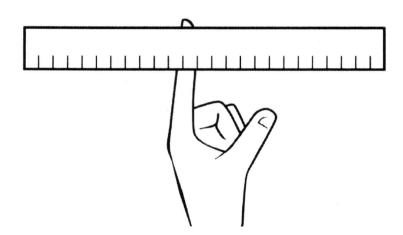

2. Mark the center of gravity with a small piece of masking tape. Write "1" on the masking tape.
3. Place an eraser 1 in. (3 cm) from the end of the ruler and tape it in place.

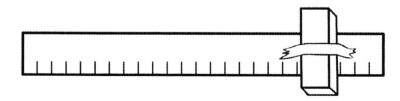

4. Repeat steps 1 and 2. This time, mark the center of gravity with a piece of masking tape with "2" written on it.

## "Experiment: Center of Gravity"—Think About It!

**1.** The ruler had a different center of gravity in each test. Use the drawings of rulers on page 54. Mark the center of gravity you found each time.

**2.** What would happen if two erasers were taped to one end of the ruler? Would the center of gravity be in the same place? Explain your thinking.

_____

_____

_____

_____

**3.** A circus acrobat does a balancing act. She balances plates on a pole. Mark where you think the center of gravity is on the pole. Draw the acrobat holding the pole.

**Try It!**

Tape an eraser over the 6 in. (15 cm) mark on the ruler. Where do you think the center of gravity will be? Try balancing the ruler. Was your prediction correct?

# Center of Gravity in Structures

## Think Back—Ruler Experiment

Do you remember finding a ruler's center of gravity? The center of gravity changed when you taped an eraser to the ruler. Without the eraser, the center of gravity was in the middle of the ruler. With the eraser, the center of gravity was closer to the eraser end.

## Center of Gravity and Stability

All structures have a center of gravity. A low center of gravity makes a structure more stable. A structure with a low center of gravity will not tip over easily.

If the heaviest part is near the bottom, the center of gravity is low. If the heaviest part is near the top, the center of gravity is higher.

## Center of Gravity and Loads

A structure holds a load. The load can change where the center of gravity is. In the ruler experiment, the eraser was a load. The ruler's center of gravity changed when you added a load at one end. The center of gravity moved closer to the load.

A ladder is a structure. The person on the ladder is the load. When a person stands on the bottom step of a ladder, the center of gravity is low. The ladder is very stable. When a person stands on the top step, the center of gravity is higher. The ladder is easier to tip over.

## "Center of Gravity in Structures"—Think About It!

Look at the drawings of two vases.

A 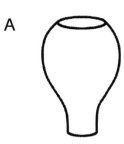     B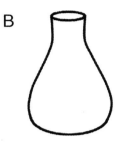

**1.** Which vase has a lower center of gravity? Tell how you know.

_____

_____

_____

_____

**2.** Which vase would tip over more easily? Why?

_____

_____

_____

_____

**3.** Pablo got a new bookcase. The bookcase came with this safety message:
"When you fill the shelves with books, fill the bottom shelves first and the top
shelves last." What could happen if Pablo fills the top shelf first? Explain why.

_____

_____

_____

_____

# Tension and Compression

## Tension

When you pull an elastic band, it stretches. Each hand pulls in a different direction. The elastic band gets longer.

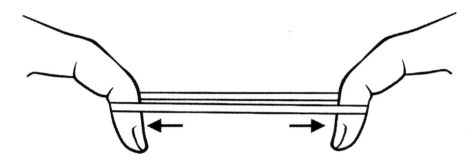

Tension is a pulling force that makes part of a structure longer.

## Compression

Compression is a pushing force. You see compression when you push down on a sponge. Compression makes objects shorter in the direction that you push.

Compression is a pushing force that makes part of a structure shorter.

## Compression and Tension in Structures

It is easy to see how tension changes an elastic band. You can see the elastic stretch. It is also easy to see a sponge get compressed. Compression and tension change structures, too. But the change is so small that the change is hard to see.

## "Tension and Compression"—Think About It!

You play tug-of-war. One team pulls on one end of a rope, while the other team pulls on the other end.

**1.** Which force acts on the rope during tug-of-war—tension or compression? How do you know?

_____

_____

_____

_____

**2.** What happens to the length of the rope during tug-of-war?

_____

_____

A table is a structure. The weight of the tabletop pushes down on the legs. The table's legs must be strong enough to hold the weight of the tabletop.

**3.** What force acts on the table's legs—tension or compression? How do you know?

_____

_____

_____

_____

**4.** When you push down on a block of wood, the block gets a tiny bit shorter. You cannot see the change. When you push down just as hard on a sponge, you can see it get shorter. Why does the sponge get shorter than the wood?

_____

_____

_____

_____

# Building a Roof

Most houses have a roof shaped like a triangle. A triangle is a strong shape that can hold a heavy load. Workers start making a roof by building a frame of wooden triangles.

The outside of the roof will be covered with large boards. The boards are then covered with shingles. The boards and shingles are heavy. The frame has to be strong enough to hold them up.

When weight pushes down on the struts (beams) of the roof, the corners of the roof are pushed out. A tie holds the bottom corners of each triangle in place. The tie makes the roof much stronger, so it will not collapse.

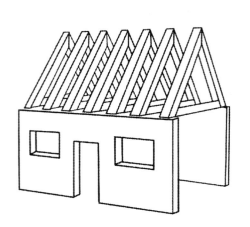

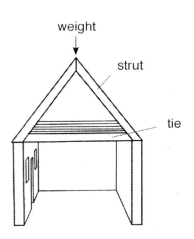

**Try It!**

Fold a strip of construction paper or thin cardboard into three equal parts to form a triangle shape. Stand the triangle up so the opening is at a bottom corner. Imagine the triangle is roof struts that are not attached to a tie. Push down on the top of the triangle. What happens? Push gently down on the two sides of the triangle at the same time. What happens? Now tape the opening together so it makes a complete triangle. Push on the top and sides again, the same way as before. This shows how a tie makes a roof stronger.

## "Building a Roof"—Think About It!

**1.** Houses built in snowy places need strong roofs. What load might those roofs have to hold up?

_____

_____

**2.** The shingles on a roof might last 20 to 25 years. They will then need to be replaced. What extra load will the roof have to hold up while shingles are being replaced?

_____

_____

_____

**3.** Explain how a tie makes a roof structure stronger.

_____

_____

_____

_____

_____

_____

**4.** The weight of shingles pushes down on a roof. Does this pushing force create tension or compression? Tell how you know.

_____

_____

_____

_____

_____

_____

# Structures Word Search

Complete the sentences below. Then, turn to the next page and find each word you filled in on the word search.

**1.** A structure is built to do something. A structure has a

_____ .

**2.** A spider builds a structure called a _____ .

**3.** A chair is a structure. The person who sits on the chair is the

_____ .

**4.** A structure is _____ when the structure can keep its

balance.

**5.** A _____ building material will last for a long time.

**6.** To build a stable structure, make sure the structure has a low

_____ of _____ .

**7.** A roof shaped like a triangle has a frame made of two types of pieces. The side piece

is the _____ . The bottom pieces are the

_____ .

**8.** A _____ material can bend without breaking.

**9.** _____ is a pulling force. It makes part of a structure longer.

continued next page ☞

Find and circle the words you wrote in the blanks on page 62.

| B | E | V | G | A | I | S | P | D | Y | C | O |
|---|---|---|---|---|---|---|---|---|---|---|---|
| F | L | O | A | D | S | T | A | B | L | E | L |
| A | B | D | V | S | O | R | H | I | A | F | M |
| S | I | G | I | H | D | U | R | A | B | L | E |
| O | X | I | R | C | O | T | X | E | W | O | S |
| I | E | T | L | A | E | Y | B | I | E | G | O |
| M | L | A | O | Z | V | N | A | T | B | F | P |
| A | F | B | Y | O | G | I | T | S | A | E | R |
| T | E | N | S | I | O | N | T | E | Z | T | U |
| E | K | I | W | C | N | J | X | Y | R | U | P |

## Amazing Structures Facts

- It took hundreds of workers about 20 years to build the Great Pyramid in Egypt. The CN Tower in Canada was built in less than four years.
- When the Great Pyramid was built, it was the tallest structure ever created by humans. When people finally built a taller structure, the Great Pyramid was more than 3,800 years old.
- Bald eagles are large birds that build huge nests. The largest bald eagle nest ever found was almost 10 ft. (3 m) wide and 20 ft. (6 m) deep.
- Trees are some of the most amazing structures found in nature. The tallest trees can grow to be more than 328 ft. (100 m) tall—that is taller than a building with 30 floors.

# Structures Collage

Cut and paste magazine pictures to create a collage of structures.

On one half of the page, paste only structures from nature.

On the other half of the page, paste only structures people make.

**Structures from Nature**

**Structures People Make**

# Why Is Soil Important?

Here is a riddle for you: *You can find me all over Earth.*
*I am usually dark brown. Plants grow in me. What am I?*

If your answer is "dirt," you are right! Scientists call dirt soil.
Keep reading to find out why soil is very important.

## Food for People and Animals

Many of the foods we eat come from plants. Fruits and vegetables come from plants.
Plants need soil to grow.

Many animals get their food from plants. For example, squirrels eat nuts that grow on
trees. Trees cannot grow without soil.

Some animals give us food. You probably know that milk comes from cows. Cows like
to eat lots of grass, and grass needs soil to grow. If cows did not have grass to eat, they
could not make milk.

## Useful Materials

We get many useful materials from plants. From trees, we get wood for building homes
and furniture. Scientists use some plants to make medicines. Without soil, trees and
other plants could not grow.

We even use soil to make useful things. Clay is a special type of soil. We use clay to
make dishes such as plates, bowls, and mugs.

## Our Beautiful Earth

Plants make Earth beautiful. Forests, fields, and gardens are all places where plants
grow. Without soil, trees could not grow in forests and grass could not grow in fields.
We need soil to grow the flowers in a garden. The plants that make Earth beautiful
need soil.

# "Why Is Soil Important?"—Think About It!

1. Think of an outdoor place you know where plants grow. Maybe the place is your backyard, a park, or the schoolyard. List the plants that grow in the soil.

   The place I chose: _____

   Plants that grow there: _____

   _____

   _____

   _____

2. Tell two ways that soil helps people have food.

   _____

   _____

   _____

   _____

3. List three things in your classroom that are made of wood.

   _____

   _____

4. Why do we need soil to have things made of wood?

   _____

   _____

   _____

   _____

5. List four foods that come from plants growing in soil. (Remember that trees are plants.)

   _____

   _____

# What Is Soil Made Of?

Soil is made of many things. We can put these things
in two groups: living things and nonliving things.

## Living Things in Soil

Did you know that soil is full
of living things? If you dig in
garden soil, you will probably
see worms. If you look very
closely, you might see tiny
insects, too. There are many
more living things in soil. Many
are too small to see.

Bacteria are tiny creatures
that live in soil. Bacteria are
so tiny that you need to use a
microscope to see them. In one
handful of soil, there might be
thousands and thousands of tiny
bacteria.

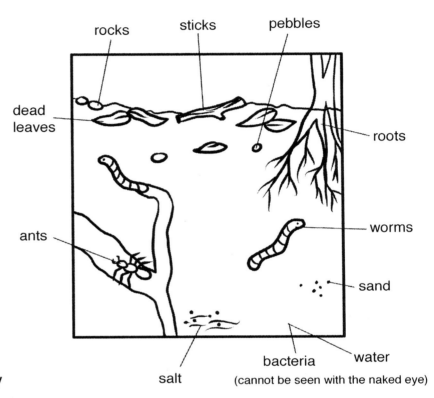

## Nonliving Things in Soil

Nonliving things are no longer alive or were never alive. Water and air are two nonliving
things in soil. You probably will not see water in soil. When soil feels moist, there is water
in it. You can not see air, but there is air in soil. Air fills the tiny spaces in soil.

Rock is another nonliving part of soil. You may find large rocks or small pebbles in soil.
Soil also contains tiny pieces of rock, such as sand.

Sometimes people put nonliving things into soil. They add fertilizer to soil to help plants
grow. They spray plants to kill harmful insects. Some of that spray goes into the soil.
They put salt on roads and sidewalks to melt the winter ice. That salt ends up in the soil.

## "What Is Soil Made Of?"—Think About It!

**1.** Each thing in the list is found in soil. Write each thing in the correct column of the chart.

| dead leaves | ants | air | water | roots | pebbles |
| bacteria | sand | rock | worms | sticks | salt |

| Living Things | Nonliving Things |
| --- | --- |
| | |

**2.** Where in soil do you find air?

_____

_____

_____

**3.** Write two facts you have learned from the text.

_____

_____

_____

# Soil Particles

## What Is a Particle?

A particle is a very small piece of something. If you look closely at sand, you will see that it is made of many very small pieces of rock. Each piece is a particle.

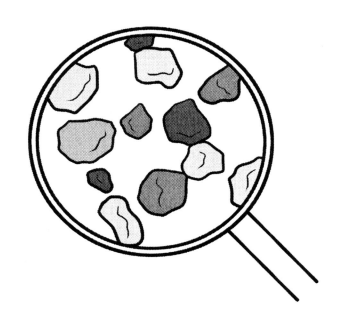

Soil contains three types of particles—sand, silt, and clay.

**Sand:** One particle of sand looks tiny, but sand particles are some of the larger particles in soil.

**Silt:** Silt is made of particles that are much smaller than sand particles. Most mud is made of particles of silt.

**Clay:** Clay particles are even smaller than silt particles. You would need a microscope to see one particle of clay.

## What Is Texture?

Texture is the way something feels. Sandpaper has a rough texture. Glass has a smooth texture. Sand, silt, and clay all have different textures. When you rub each one between your fingers, they all feel different.

| Particle | Texture |
|----------|---------|
| Sand | When you rub sand between your fingers, you can feel the hard particles. This has a gritty texture. |
| Silt | Silt particles have a smooth texture, like powder. This is because silt particles are much smaller than sand particles. |
| Clay | Dry clay particles stick together. Dry clay is hard like cement. Wet clay has a smooth and slippery texture. |

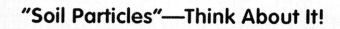

## "Soil Particles"—Think About It!

1. Other things are made up of particles. You can see some particles when you look closely. Circle the things in the list that have particles you can see.

   **sugar**      **milk**           **salt**

   **butter**     **ketchup**        **powdered drink mix**

2. You have five senses. Circle the sense you use to find out the texture of something.

   **sight**    **smell**    **touch**       **hearing**     **taste**

3. Clay, sand, and silt are three types of particles in soil. Write the particles in order from smallest to largest.

| Smallest | Medium | Largest |
|----------|--------|---------|
|          |        |         |

4. Imagine you have three cups the same size. You fill one cup with silt, one cup with clay, and one cup with sand.

   Which cup contains the most particles? Give a reason for your answer.

   _____

   _____

   _____

   _____

5. You have one dish with silt particles in it. Another dish contains sand particles. How can you compare the texture of the two types of particles?

   _____

   _____

   _____

   _____

   _____

# Air and Water in Soil

Plant roots need to get air and water from soil. Where can you find air and water in soil? Remember that soil is made up of particles.

## The Spaces Between Particles

Imagine you have one clear plastic cup filled with stones. Another cup is filled with sand. You can see spaces between the stones in the cup. Think of the stones as large particles. Large particles do not fit closely together. There are large spaces between the particles.

Sand particles are much smaller than stones. Small particles fit closely together. They leave only tiny spaces between particles. The particles of sand are so close together that you cannot see the tiny spaces between the particles.

The spaces between large particles are larger than the spaces between small particles.

**large particles**

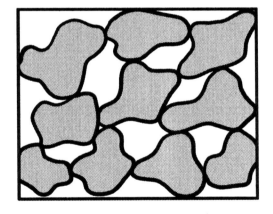

**small particles**

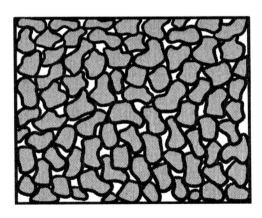

In soil, you can find air and water in the spaces between particles.

## Soil Particles

Remember that sand, silt, and clay particles are all different sizes. Sand particles are larger than silt particles. The spaces between sand particles are larger than the spaces between silt particles.

When there are larger spaces between particles, more air and water can fill the spaces.

## "Air and Water in Soil"—Think About It!

**Use this story to answer questions 1 and 2.**

Zara has two cups that are the same size. She fills one cup with large stones. The other cup she fills with small stones. Zara wonders how much water can fit in each cup. She pours water to fill each cup. Then she pours out the water from each cup and measures it in a measuring cup.

**1.** Which cup held the most water—the cup with the small stones or the cup with large stones?

_____

_____

**2.** Each cup was full of stones before Zara added water. Where did the water go when Zara filled the cups?

_____

_____

**Use this story to answer questions 3 and 4.**

Tim has two cups that are the same size. One cup is filled with clay particles. The other is filled with silt particles. Tim knows that there is also air in each cup.

**3.** Both cups are filled with particles. Where is the air in the cups?

_____

_____

**4.** Which cup has the most air in it? Tell how you know.

_____

_____

_____

_____

# Experiment: What Is in This Soil?

Try this experiment to find out what is in a sample of soil.

## What You Need

- A clear jar with straight sides (not too small)
- Enough soil to fill the jar halfway
- Water
- A spoon or stirring stick

## What You Do

1. Add dirt to the jar almost halfway. Notice how the dirt looks.

2. **Slowly** add water to the jar until the jar is almost full. Watch for several moments. Do you see any bubbles rising from the dirt?

3. Stir the water and dirt to mix them together.

4. Leave the jar for 2 or 3 hours. Do not touch or move the jar.

5. When the water at the top clears, take a close look at the soil. (Do not move the jar or you might mix up the soil and water again.)

## "Experiment: What Is in This Soil?"—Think About It!

**1.** Did you see any bubbles after you added water to the soil?

_____

**2.** What would make bubbles that rise from soil?

_____

_____

_____

**3.** How did the dirt look before you added water? How did it look after 2 to 3 hours? Write any differences you noticed.

_____

_____

_____

_____

_____

**What Happened?**

- After you stirred the water and dirt, dirt particles settled into layers.
- The largest and heaviest particles of dirt fell to the bottom of the jar. These made the bottom layer. You should see small stones in the sand at the bottom.
- The layer above the sand and stones is made of silt. Silt particles are smaller and lighter than sand particles.
- If you see a layer above the silt, it is made of clay particles. Clay particles are smaller and lighter than silt particles.
- Were there any bits and pieces of plants in your soil? These sit on the top layer. They may float at the top the water.
- Does the water above the dirt look cloudy? If it does, that probably means clay particles are floating in the water.

# Air and Water for Plant Roots

## Watering Plants

When you water an indoor plant, the water goes on top of the soil then moves down into the soil. If you add lots of water, some of the water will come out of holes in the bottom of the pot. The soil will feel damp for a few days, so we know that some of the water stays in the soil. We say that the soil holds the water.

When it rains, or when you water a garden, the water moves into the soil. The soil at the top of the garden stays damp for a while, so we know that this soil is holding some of the water. The rest of the water sinks deeper and deeper into the soil.

## How Does Water Move Through Soil?

Water moves through the spaces in soil. The spaces are between the particles. Water can move quickly through soil when there are large spaces between the particles. Water moves more slowly through smaller spaces between the particles.

## How Do Plants Get Air and Water from Soil?

Plant roots grow down into soil. The roots need both air and water from the soil. Air and water are in the spaces between soil particles. If the spaces fill with water, how do the roots get air?

Remember that water moves down through soil. Water moves through the spaces between the particles. Water gets stuck in some spaces, so the soil stays damp. The rest of the water moves deeper into the soil, leaving empty spaces higher up. Some spaces hold water and others are filled with air. The plant roots get both air and water.

# "Air and Water for Plant Roots"—Think About It!

1. Some indoor plants will die if you water them every day. Think of the spaces in the soil. What is stopped from happening when the soil contains too much water?

_____

_____

_____

_____

**Use this story to answer questions 2, 3, and 4.**

Abdul and Tina have two paper cups. They make four holes in the bottom of each cup. Abdul fills his cup halfway with small stones. Tina fills her cup halfway with sand. They pour the same amount of water into each cup. Then they watch to see which cup the water flows through faster.

2. Are the spaces between the particles larger in the cup of small stones or in the cup of sand?

_____

3. Which cup will water flow through faster? Why?

_____

_____

_____

_____

4. Imagine Abdul's cup had silt in it and Tina's cup had clay. Which cup would the water flow through faster? Explain why.

_____

_____

_____

_____

# Nutrients in Soil

## What Are Nutrients?

Nutrients are substances that people, plants, and animals need to grow and stay healthy. Vitamins are examples of nutrients that people need. We get nutrients from the foods we eat.

## Where Do Plants Get Nutrients?

Plants get nutrients from living things in the soil. The living things give nutrients back to the soil when they decompose. Their waste gives nutrients to the soil, too. Animal droppings are nonliving things, but they come from live animals. Animals leave their droppings on the ground, where they get mixed into soil.

## How Do Plants Get Nutrients from Soil?

A plant root cannot take in droppings or a dead worm. So how do plants get nutrients from the soil?

Bacteria in the soil feed on dead creatures, such as a dead worm. As the bacteria eat, they free nutrients from the dead creature's body. Those nutrients mix into the soil.

People put nutrients into soil when they use fertilizer in their gardens. Fertilizer helps plants grow because it is full of nutrients.

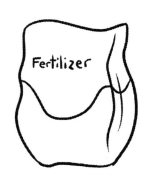

The nutrients in soil mix with water. When plant roots take in water, they also take in nutrients. When the soil is too dry, plants cannot take in the nutrients from the soil. Plants will die if they do not get enough nutrients.

## "Nutrients in Soil"—Think About It!

1. Marco was digging in his garden. In the soil, he found the things listed below. Put a check mark beside the nonliving things.

   ❏ a plant's roots              ❏ a stone

   ❏ a piece of a plastic bag    ❏ a nail

   ❏ a beetle                     ❏ a piece of broken glass

   ❏ a bone his dog buried       ❏ an sprouting seed

2. People put fertilizer on gardens. They often mix fertilizer into the top layer of soil. Plant roots are in deeper layers of soil. How do the nutrients in the fertilizer get down to the roots?

   _____

   _____

   _____

   _____

3. How do bacteria in soil help keep plants healthy?

   _____

   _____

   _____

   _____

4. When some people cut their grass, they leave the grass clippings on the lawn. Why do grass clippings help lawns grow?

   _____

   _____

   _____

   _____

# Three Types of Soil

Most soil contains three types of particles: sand, silt, and clay. These different types of particles create different types of soil.

Sandy soil is made mostly of sand particles. Water soaks quickly down through this type of soil. (When water runs quickly through soil, we say that the soil drains quickly.) If you squeeze sandy soil in your hand, it does not stick together well.

**Sandy:** mostly sand particles

Loam has equal amounts of sand, silt, and clay particles. Water drains from this type of soil more slowly than from sandy soil. If you squeeze loamy soil in your hand, it sticks together fairly well.

**Loam:** equal amounts of sand, silt, and clay particles

Clay soil is made mostly of clay particles. Water drains very slowly from this type of soil. If you squeeze clay soil, it sticks together very well.

**Clay:** mostly clay particles

## Water, Air, and Nutrients

Plants need water, air, and nutrients. Nutrients in soil mix with water. Plants get nutrients when their roots take in water.

If water drains from soil too quickly, plant roots do not have much time to take in water and nutrients. Plants will not grow well in soil that drains too quickly.

If water drains from soil too slowly, the spaces between soil particles stay filled with water for a long time. Plant roots will have a lot of time to take in water and nutrients. Some plants grow very well in swamps, lakes, and rivers. Other plants do not grow well in soil that is too wet.

# "Three Types of Soil"—Think About It!

**Use this story to answer questions 1 to 3.**

The plants in Tony's garden are not growing well. After it rains, the soil stays wet for a long time. Tony wonders if the soil in his garden is not good for plants. He squeezes some of the soil in his hand, and it makes a ball that does not crumble apart.

**1.** What type of soil is in Tony's garden? Tell how you know.

_____

_____

_____

_____

**2.** Why are Tony's plants not growing well?

_____

_____

_____

**3.** What type of soil would help the plants in Tony's garden grow better? Why?

_____

_____

_____

_____

**4.** Sarah's plant is not growing well in sandy soil. What do the roots of this plant need more of—air or water? Tell how you know.

_____

_____

_____

_____

# Wonderful Worms!

The next time you see a worm, say "Thank you!" Why? Worms help soil and plants in many ways.

## Worm Castings

Worm waste is called castings. What is so great about worm castings? They are great fertilizer for plants.

Worms eat soil because it contains pieces of things that were living. (There are a lot of nutrients in dead things.) The castings that worms leave behind are full of nutrients. The nutrients in castings mix easily with water. Plant roots can take in the nutrients that are mixed in that water.

Worms sometimes come out of the ground. They can bite grass and drag it underground to eat. Worms help put more living things into the soil.

## Worm Tunnels

Worms make tunnels as they move through soil. The tunnels fill with air.

Worm tunnels bring more air to different parts of the soil. Plant roots need air, so worm tunnels are good for plants.

Worm tunnels can also help water drain through soil. Water can run quickly through worm tunnels. The tunnels help to bring water deep into the soil. This is especially helpful to plants growing in soil that drains slowly.

Now you know why gardeners are happy to find worms in garden soil. The worms make the soil better for growing plants.

# "Wonderful Worms!"—Think About It!

1. Think about worm tunnels. Think about soil that drains slowly. How can worm tunnels help soil that drains slowly?

_____

_____

_____

_____

2. Pushing roots through soil is hard work for a plant. How do worm tunnels help plant roots?

_____

_____

_____

_____

3. Worms eat dead things in soil. How does that help plants?

_____

_____

_____

_____

_____

**Did You Know?**

Worms feel slimy because their skin makes a slippery coating. This coating makes it easier for worms to move through the soil.

# How Nature Recycles

People recycle garbage. Did you know that nature recycles, too?

## Step 1

Dead leaves, twigs, and pine needles fall to the ground. Bacteria in the soil eat them. The bacteria free nutrients in the dead plant material. These nutrients go back into the soil.

Worms carry small pieces of dead plant material underground to eat. Worm castings have nutrients from the digested dead plant material. The nutrients in worm castings mix into the soil.

## Step 2

Nutrients in the soil mix with water. Plant roots take in nutrients when they take in water.

## Step 3

Plants grow larger when they get water, air, and nutrients from the soil. Some parts of the plants die. Leaves, twigs, and pine needles die and fall to the ground. Then the cycle starts over again.

## Think About It!

1. People water their gardens. They add fertilizer to put nutrients into the soil.
   No one waters or fertilizes the forest. Why do forest plants grow so well?

   _____

   _____

   _____

   _____

   _____

   _____

# Composting

Reduce, reuse, and recycle by composting!

Composting is the process of recycling decomposed (broken down) natural waste. Natural waste includes things such as leaves, or fruit and vegetable scraps. Over time, the natural waste will decompose into a rich soil called compost. Compost can be spread into flowerbeds, dug into vegetable gardens, spread under trees and bushes, or sprinkled on the lawn. Compost can be used anywhere that you want to give a boost of nutrients to the soil.

Good places to set up a compost bin are any place near a garden, and close to a source of water. This way you can easily add to the compost and keep it moist. A workforce of bacteria, earthworms, and other organisms, work to break down the natural waste. This workforce needs air and water to live and work.

Look at the table to see what can and cannot go into a compost bin.

| Examples of what you can put in the compost bin. | Examples of what you cannot put in the compost bin. |
|---|---|
| • leaves<br>• grass<br>• small garden clippings<br>• pine needles<br>• wood ash<br>• bark<br>• nutshells<br>• fruit and vegetable peels or seeds<br>• coffee grounds, including the paper filter<br>• tea bags<br>• sawdust<br>• shredded or torn-up newspaper<br>• paper towels<br>• napkins | • meat<br>• fish<br>• bones<br>• dairy products<br>• vegetable oils<br>• fats<br>• human or pet waste<br>• charcoal ash<br>• plastic<br>• glass<br>• aluminum foil<br>• plastic wrap<br>• plastic bags<br>• Styrofoam |

## "Composting"—Think About It!

1. How does composting help people to reduce, reuse, and recycle? Use information from the text and your own ideas to explain your thinking.

_____

_____

_____

_____

_____

_____

_____

_____

_____

_____

_____

_____

2. On a separate piece of paper, design an information poster to encourage people to compost. Place a check in the box next to each item after it has been completed.

❑ My poster has a title that can be read from 3 ft. (1 m) away.

❑ My poster includes at least three reasons to compost.

❑ My printing is neat and easy to read.

❑ I checked the spelling.

❑ I checked the grammar.

❑ My poster is attractive and includes pictures.

# George Washington Carver

George Washington Carver was a scientist and inventor. Sometimes he was called "the farmer's best friend."

## Growing Up

George was born in the 1860s in Missouri. Like his parents, George was a slave. Child slaves had to work hard on farms. George was often sick and too weak to work on a farm. He went to school instead.

George was a very good student. He liked science most of all. He went to university and became an expert on plants. Later, he went to teach at a university in Alabama.

## Helping Farmers

Many farmers in Alabama grew cotton. As cotton grows, it takes lots of nutrients from the soil. After a few years, the soil does not have enough nutrients to grow strong, healthy cotton plants. George found a way to solve this problem.

George discovered that peanut and pea plants put nutrients back into the soil. He told farmers not to grow cotton in the same field every year. He said to plant peas or peanuts some years to give the soil more nutrients. The next year, farmers could grow cotton in that field again.

George invented many new ways for people to use the plants farmers grew. Peanut butter is one of his most famous inventions. He also discovered how to make paint from soybeans.

George died on January 5, 1943. Each year, the United States celebrates January 5 as George Washington Carver Day.

## "George Washington Carver"—Think About It!

**1.** How was George's life as a child different from the lives of other child slaves?

_____

_____

_____

**2.** What problem did farmers have when they grew cotton every year in the same field?

_____

_____

_____

**3.** How did planting peas or peanuts help farmers who grew cotton?

_____

_____

_____

**4.** Why was George called "the farmer's best friend"?

_____

_____

_____

**5.** How do you know that Americans think George Washington Carver is an important person in American history?

_____

_____

_____

# Soil Review

**1.** List three living things found in soil.

_____

**2.** List at least three nonliving things found in soil.

_____

_____

**3.** There are three types of particles in soil. List them from smallest to largest.

_____

**4.** How do plants take in nutrients from soil?

_____

_____

**5.** Which type of soil is best for most plants? Is it clay soil, loam, or sand? Tell why.

_____

_____

_____

_____

**6.** How do worm tunnels help soil and plants? List two ways.
(Can you remember a third way?)

_____

_____

_____

_____

# STEM-Related Occupations

To learn more about some of these occupations visit the following websites:

www.sciencebuddies.org/science-engineering-careers

https://kids.usa.gov/watch-videos/index.shtml

Accountant
Aerospace Engineer
Agricultural Engineer
Agricultural Technician
Aircraft Mechanic and
    Service Technician
Animal Breeder
Animal Trainer
Animator
Anthropologist
Architect
Astronaut
Astronomer
Athletic Trainer
Audio Engineer
Audiologist
Automotive Mechanic
Biochemical Engineer
Biochemist/Biophysicist
Biologist
Biology Teacher
Biomedical Engineer
Business Owner
Cardiovascular Technician
Carpenter
Chef
Chemical Engineer
Chemical Technician
Chemistry Teacher
Chiropractor
Civil Engineer
Civil Engineering Technician
Climate Change Analyst
Clinical Psychologist
Computer Engineer
Computer Programmer
Computer Systems Analyst
Construction Manager
Counselling Psychologist
Dietetic Technician

Dietitian and Nutritionist
Doctor
Electrical Engineering Technician
Electrician
Electronics Engineer
Emergency Medical Technician
Environmental Engineer
Environmental Engineering Technician
Environmental Restoration Planner
Environmental Scientist
Epidemiologist
Fire-Prevention Engineer
Fish and Game Worker
Food Science Technician
Food Scientist and Technologist
Forest and Conservation Technician
Forest and Conservation Worker
Geoscientist
Graphic Designer
Hydrologist
Industrial Engineer
Interior Designer
Landscape Architect
Manufacturing Engineer
Marine Architect
Marine Biologist
Math Teacher
Mechanical Engineer
Mechanical Engineering Technician
Medical Lab Technician
Medical Scientist
Meteorologist
Microbiologist
Microsystems Engineer
Mining and Geological Engineer
Molecular and Cellular Biologist
Neurologist
Nuclear Engineer
Nursery and Greenhouse Manager
Nutritionist

Occupational Health and Safety Specialist
Optical Engineer
Optometrist
Paleontologist
Patent Lawyer
Pathologist
Park Ranger
Petroleum Engineer
Pharmacist
Physical Therapist
Physician
Physician Assistant
Physicist
Pilot
Psychologist
Registered Nurse
Respiratory Therapist
Robotics Engineer
Robotics Technician
School Psychologist
Seismologist
Software Developer (Applications)
Software Developer (Systems Software)
Soil and Plant Scientist
Soil and Water Conservationist
Space Scientist
Speech-Language Pathologist
Statistician
Transportation Engineer
Transportation Planner
Urban Planner
Veterinarian
Video Game Designer
Volcanologist
Water/Wastewater Engineer
Wind Energy Engineer
X-ray Technician
Zookeeper
Zoologist
Wildlife Biologist

# Early Engineers: The Wright Brothers

The Wright brothers were Orville and Wilbur. They built and flew the first plane. They made the first flight on record in 1903. Over the years, they worked to make better planes. Their work helped others make the planes we see today.

## Early Life

Orville and Wilbur read many books. They loved to work on science projects. They made a printing press. Then they opened a bicycle shop. These projects helped them become better designers.

They made a heavier-than-air plane called the Wright Flyer. It had a light engine. They made the plane so they could control it in the air.

## The First Flight

In 1903, they flew their plane at Kitty Hawk, North Carolina. Kitty Hawk had sand dunes so they could land softly. Orville was the pilot. Wilbur ran beside the wing. The first flight lasted 12 seconds at a speed of 7 miles (11 kilometers) per hour!

Over the years, they made better planes. In 1908, the brothers made their longest flight. It was 2 hours and 19 minutes long.

You can visit the Wright Flyer in the National Air and Space Museum in Washington, D.C.

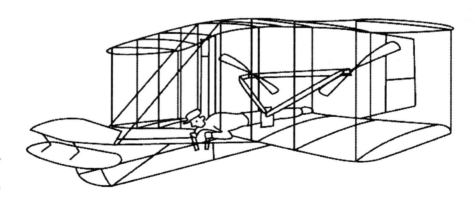

The Wright Flyer had a wooden frame covered with fabric. It had an engine, too.

# Early Engineers: "The Wright Brothers"—Think About It!

**1.** What is the most important event in this text? How do you know?

_____

_____

_____

**2.** How did Orville and Wilbur become better designers?

_____

_____

_____

**3.** Why did the Wright brothers choose Kitty Hawk, North Carolina as the place to fly their plane?

_____

_____

**4.** Why do you think the Wright brothers were able to invent the first plane? What details in the text give you this information?

_____

_____

_____

**5.** If you could interview the Wright brothers, what would you ask about?

_____

_____

_____

# Early Engineers: Alexander Graham Bell

Alexander Graham Bell was an inventor. His most famous invention is the telephone.

## Early Life

Alexander was born in Scotland in 1847. As a young boy, he loved doing experiments to learn new things. He made his first invention when he was 12 years old. It was a machine that helped turn wheat into flour.

## Leaving Scotland

Alexander and his parents moved to Canada in 1870. They bought a farm near Brantford, Ontario. Alexander set up a workshop where he could make inventions. He called the workshop his dreaming place.

Alexander did many experiments with electricity and sound. Then he got a job as a teacher in Boston, Massachusetts. Alexander taught deaf children how to speak. He still had time to work on inventions.

## Inventing the Telephone

Alexander wanted to invent a machine that could send voices through a wire. Then someone could talk with a person who was far away. Alexander worked very hard and finally invented the telephone.

## After the Telephone

Alexander returned to Canada. He did many more experiments and made more inventions. He liked doing experiments with kites to learn how things fly.

## Early Engineers: "Alexander Graham Bell"—Think About It!

**1.** How do you know that Alexander was curious when he was a boy?

_____

_____

_____

**2.** Alexander's workshop was not a place to sleep. Why do you think he called the workshop his dreaming place? Use information from the text and your own ideas.

_____

_____

_____

_____

_____

**3.** Alexander was very interested in sound. How did he work with sound in his teaching job?

_____

_____

_____

**4.** In Alexander's telephone, how did the speaker's voice get to the listener?

_____

_____

_____

# Early Inventions: Telephones from the Past

Most people use a telephone every day. A telephone lets us talk to people who are far away. The telephone has changed a lot in the last 100 years. Let's look at some telephones from the past.

**100 Years Ago**

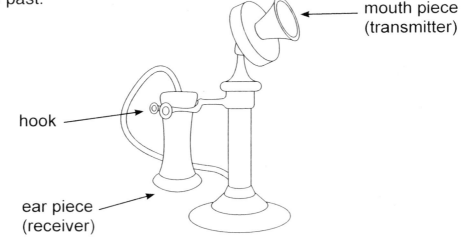

mouth piece
(transmitter)

hook

ear piece
(receiver)

This telephone is called a candlestick telephone. People held the receiver to their ear to hear. They spoke into the transmitter at the top of the phone.

To make a call, people tapped the hook. A person called a telephone operator answered. The person then told the operator the telephone number they wanted to call.

**75 years ago**

handset

receiver

transmitter

rotary dial

This telephone is called a rotary telephone. People used the handset to talk and listen. They used the rotary dial to call a telephone number.

continued next page

How did people use the dial to call a telephone number with a rotary telephone?

| | |
|---|---|
| **Step 1**<br>The caller put their finger in the hole over the number they wanted to dial.<br>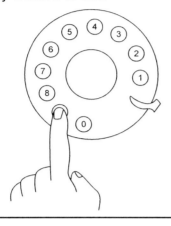 | **Step 2**<br>They used their finger to push the dial around as far to the right as it would go.<br>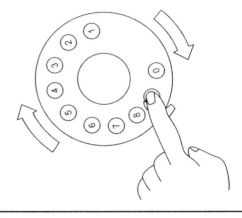 |
| **Step 3**<br>They pulled their finger out of the hole. The dial moved back to where it was when they started.<br>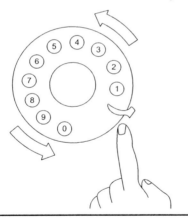 | **Step 4**<br>The caller then repeated Steps 1, 2, and 3 for the next number in the telephone number. They repeated the steps until the whole telephone number was dialed.<br>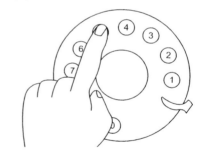 |

## 45 Years Ago

This telephone is called a push-button telephone. This telephone did not have a dial. People pushed the buttons with numbers on them to call someone.

## Early Inventions: "Telephones from the Past"—Think About It!

**1.** Look at the picture of a candlestick telephone. How do you think this telephone got its name?

_____

_____

_____

**2.** What is the name of the part of a rotary phone that people held in their hand? Tell where you found the answer.

_____

_____

_____

**3.** Think of the different phones from long ago. Which phone would you like to try using? Tell why.

_____

_____

_____

**4.** Think about the cell phones people use now. Tell one way that a cell phone is different from a rotary phone.

_____

_____

**5.** What other special features do cell phones have?

_____

_____

_____

# New Inventions: The Clean Water Book

How do we get water for drinking and cooking? We turn on the tap. The water that comes out is clean. There are no germs in it.

In some countries, people do not have taps in their homes. They might get water from a lake or a river. The water might be dirty and have germs in it. Germs can make people sick.

Teri Dankovich is a scientist. She invented an easy way for people to make dirty water clean. What is her invention? It is a special kind of book.

How can a book make dirty water clean? The pages of the book are made of special paper. Inside the paper are tiny pieces of silver or copper. The silver or copper kills germs in the water. Look below to see how people use the book to make water clean.

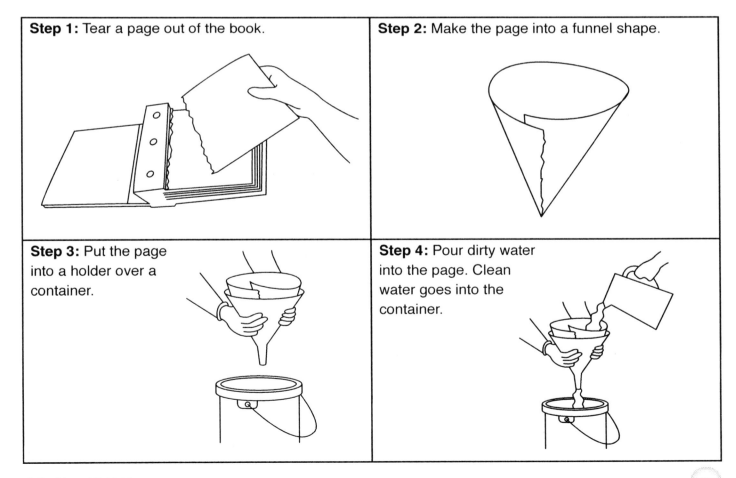

**Step 1:** Tear a page out of the book.

**Step 2:** Make the page into a funnel shape.

**Step 3:** Put the page into a holder over a container.

**Step 4:** Pour dirty water into the page. Clean water goes into the container.

# New Inventions: "The Clean Water Book"—Think About It!

**1.** How does Teri's invention help people?

_____

_____

_____

_____

**2.** Why do people not need Teri's book in your city?

_____

_____

_____

_____

**3.** Name three other inventions that use water. Think of inventions in your home.

_____

_____

_____

_____

## Brain Stretch

People use water for more than just drinking and cooking. Make a list of other ways that people use water.

_____

_____

_____

_____

# Amazing Robots

## What Is a Robot?

A robot is a machine that can do things that people do. You might see robots in movies and television shows. These robots often look a bit like people. They might have a head, eyes, a mouth, and arms. However, most robots do not look like people.

## What Can Robots Do?

Different kinds of robots can do different things. Some robots work in factories building cars. Some robots were sent to Mars to take photos of the planet. Scientists can create robots to do many different jobs.

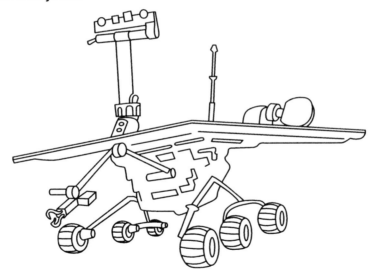

**The Mars Rover is a robot that explored Mars.**

## Why Do We Use Robots?

Robots can do some jobs faster than people can. Robots never get bored of doing the same thing over and over again.

Some robots do things that are too dangerous for people to do. For example, scientists would like to learn more about volcanoes but it is dangerous for a person to go inside them. There are robots that can explore what is happening inside a volcano. These robots take pictures for scientists to look at.

continued next page ☞

## Robots to the Rescue

What happens in an earthquake? The ground shakes and some buildings fall down. After an earthquake, a house might be only a pile of bricks and boards. People might be trapped inside! It can take a long time to move all the bricks and boards to look for people.

Scientists are building snake robots. These robots will search for people trapped inside buildings after an earthquake. A snake robot can quickly crawl through tiny spaces that people cannot get through. The robot takes photos, then comes back out. People look at the photos to see if there is anyone who needs to be rescued.

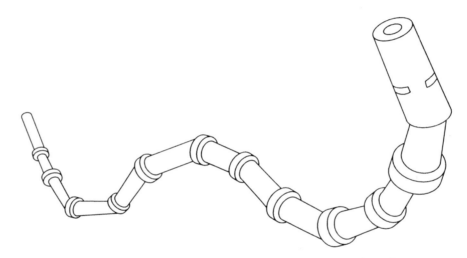

**A snake robot can help save lives after an earthquake.**

## Think About It!

1. People can buy small, round vacuum cleaners that move across a floor by themselves. All people need to do is turn them on. Do you think these vacuum cleaners are robots? Tell why or why not.

_____

_____

_____

_____

**2.** Think of a robot that you would like to create. Draw a picture of your robot. Then tell what your robot can do.

My robot can...

_____

_____

_____

_____

_____

_____

_____

# When I Grow Up...

Draw a picture of what you would like to be when you grow up.

I would like to be a _____ .

## Job Description

_____

_____

_____

I want to be this when I grow up because _____

_____

_____

_____ .

# Engineering in Our Daily Lives

Engineers design and build things that we use every day. Use magazines to cut out and paste pictures of things that engineers designed. Some examples include a toothbrush or a video game.

Write about your collage.

_____

_____

_____

# Engineers Make Our Lives Better

Cut out and paste two pictures of things that make people's lives easier. Explain your thinking.

**Complete the sentences.**

I picked a picture of

_____.

I chose this because _____

_____

_____

**Complete the sentences.**

I picked a picture of

_____.

I chose this because _____

_____

_____

# Think Like an Engineer!

An engineer is a person who designs and build things. Engineers want to understand how and why things work. Engineers try different ideas, learn from their mistakes, then try again. Engineers call these steps the design process.

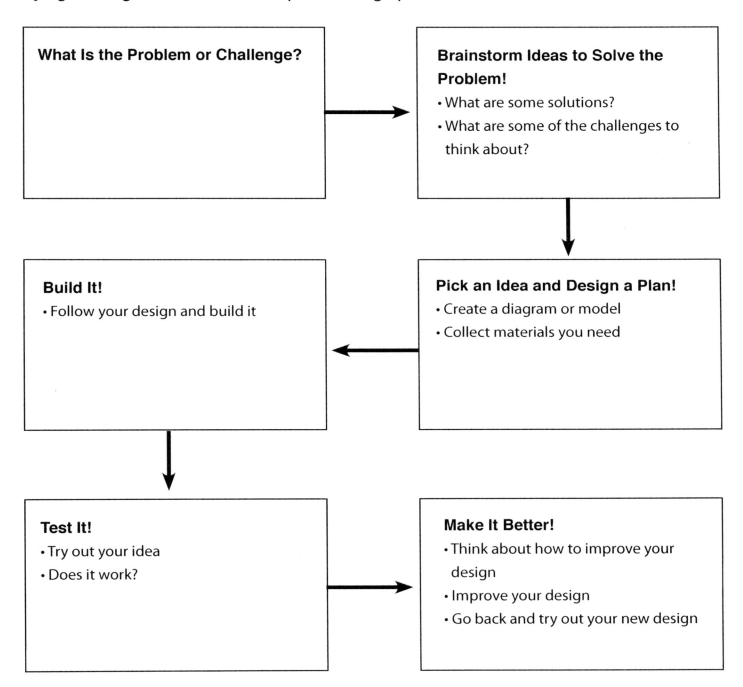

**What Is the Problem or Challenge?**

**Brainstorm Ideas to Solve the Problem!**
• What are some solutions?
• What are some of the challenges to think about?

**Build It!**
• Follow your design and build it

**Pick an Idea and Design a Plan!**
• Create a diagram or model
• Collect materials you need

**Test It!**
• Try out your idea
• Does it work?

**Make It Better!**
• Think about how to improve your design
• Improve your design
• Go back and try out your new design

Remember to be patient. Take your time to figure things out.

# The Design Process

**1.** What is the problem or challenge?

_____

_____

_____

**2.** Think about it! What are some ideas to solve the problem or challenge?

_____

_____

_____

_____

_____

_____

_____

_____

continued next page ☞

**3.** Pick a design idea! Draw and label a picture of your design. Write about your plan.

_____

_____

continued next page 👉

**4.** Get ready! What materials do you need?

| | |
|---|---|
| | |
| | |
| | |
| | |
| | |
| | |
| | |
| | |

continued next page 👉

**5.** Test it! Build your design and try it out.

Did it work?   Yes ☐   A little ☐   No ☐

**6.** Make it better! How can you make your design better?

_____

_____

_____

**7.** Try your design out again! What happened?

_____

_____

_____

**8.** What do you wonder about?

_____

_____

**9.** What are you proud of?

_____

_____

# STEM Vocabulary

## STEM Focus _____

Keep a list of new STEM words you have learned. Make sure to include the definition for each word.

| Word | Definition |
|---|---|
|  |  |
|  |  |
|  |  |
|  |  |
|  |  |
|  |  |
|  |  |
|  |  |

# How Am I Doing?

|  | Completing my work | Using my time wisely | Following directions | Keeping organized |
|---|---|---|---|---|
| **Full speed ahead!** | • My work is always complete and done with care.<br>• I added extra details to my work. | • I always get my work done on time. | • I always follow directions. | • My materials are always neatly organized.<br>• I am always prepared and ready to learn. |
| **Keep going!** | • My work is complete and done with care.<br>• I added extra details to my work. | • I usually get my work done on time. | • I usually follow directions without reminders. | • I usually can find my materials.<br>• I am usually prepared and ready to learn. |
| **Slow down!** | • My work is complete.<br>• I need to check my work. | • I sometimes get my work done on time. | • I sometimes need reminders to follow directions. | • I sometimes need time to find my materials.<br>• I am sometimes prepared and ready to learn. |
| **Stop!** | • My work is not complete.<br>• I need to check my work. | • I rarely get my work done on time. | • I need reminders to follow directions. | • I need to organize my materials.<br>• I am rarely prepared and ready to learn. |

# STEM Rubric

| | Level 1<br>Below<br>Expectations | Level 2<br>Approaches<br>Expectations | Level 3<br>Meets<br>Expectations | Level 4<br>Exceeds<br>Expectations |
|---|---|---|---|---|
| **Knowledge of STEM Concepts** | • Displays little understanding of concepts.<br><br>• Rarely gives complete explanations.<br><br>• Intensive teacher support is needed. | • Displays a satisfactory understanding of most concepts.<br><br>• Sometimes gives appropriate, but incomplete explanations.<br><br>• Teacher support is sometimes needed. | • Displays a considerable understanding of most concepts.<br><br>• Usually gives complete or nearly complete explanations.<br><br>• Infrequent teacher support is needed. | • Displays a thorough understanding of all or almost all concepts.<br><br>• Consistently gives appropriate and complete explanations independently.<br><br>• No teacher support is needed. |
| **Application of STEM Concepts** | • Relates STEM concepts to outside world with extensive teacher prompts.<br><br>• Application of concepts rarely appropriate and accurate. | • Relates STEM concepts to outside world with some teacher prompts.<br><br>• Application of concepts sometimes appropriate and accurate. | • Relates STEM concepts to outside world with few teacher prompts.<br><br>• Application of concepts usually appropriate and accurate. | • Relates STEM concepts to outside world independently.<br><br>• Application of concepts almost always appropriate and accurate. |
| **Written Communication of Ideas** | • Expresses ideas with limited critical thinking skills.<br><br>• Few ideas are well organized and effective. | • Expresses ideas with some critical thinking skills.<br><br>• Some ideas are well organized and effective. | • Expresses ideas with considerable critical thinking skills.<br><br>• Most ideas are well organized and effective. | • Expresses ideas with in-depth critical thinking skills.<br><br>• Ideas are well organized and effective. |
| **Oral Communication of Ideas** | • Rarely uses correct STEM terminology when discussing STEM concepts. | • Sometimes uses correct STEM terminology when discussing STEM concepts. | • Usually uses correct STEM terminology when discussing STEM concepts. | • Consistently uses correct STEM terminology when discussing STEM concepts. |

**Notes:** _____

_____

_____

# STEM Focus _____

| Student's Name | Knowledge of STEM Concepts | Application of STEM Concepts | Written Communication of Ideas | Oral Communication Skills | Overall Grade |
|---|---|---|---|---|---|
| | | | | | |
| | | | | | |
| | | | | | |
| | | | | | |
| | | | | | |
| | | | | | |
| | | | | | |
| | | | | | |
| | | | | | |
| | | | | | |
| | | | | | |
| | | | | | |
| | | | | | |
| | | | | | |
| | | | | | |
| | | | | | |
| | | | | | |
| | | | | | |
| | | | | | |
| | | | | | |
| | | | | | |
| | | | | | |
| | | | | | |
| | | | | | |

# STEM Expert!

_____

# Amazing work!

# Great Work!

_____

# Keep up the effort!

# Unit: Growth and Changes in Plants

## What Do Plants Need? pages 2–3

**1.**

|  | Plants | People |
|---|---|---|
| Water | X | X |
| Time to sleep |  | X |
| Air | X | X |
| Soil | X |  |
| Warmth | X | X |

**2.** Sunlight coming in the window gives the plant the light and warmth it needs.

**3.** There is not enough space for the roots to spread out.

**4.** Answers will vary.

## Parts of a Plant, pages 4–5

**1.**

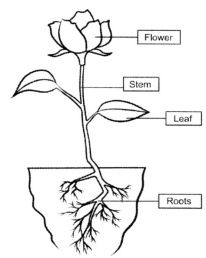

Flower

Stem

Leaf

Roots

**2.** stem

**3.** roots

**4.** flower

**5.** roots and leaf

**6.** flower

**7.** stem

**8.** flower

## Parts of a Flower, pages 6–7

**1.** Petal—more than one; Sepal—more than one; Stamen—more than one; Pistil—one

**2.** Flowers have a powder called pollen. The powder is on top of a stamen. A flower can make seeds when the powder gets to the top of the pistil.

**3.** Insects move pollen from the stamen to the pistil (pollination) so the flower can make seeds.

## Life Cycle of a Plant, pages 8–9

**1.** Labels from top: seed, sprout, seedling, adult plant, plant with fruit

## Experiment: Watching Seeds Grow, pages 10–12

**1–4.** Predictions will vary. Remind students to compare the results with their predictions at appropriate times.

**5.** The plant that grows from the seed will need light and warmth.

**6.** Sample answers: sunflower, pumpkin, nuts, strawberries, raspberries, tomato

## How Do Plants, Animals, and People Get Energy? pages 13–14

**1.** Energy first comes from sunlight.

**2.** Plants use energy to grow larger, grow flowers and fruit, and to make food for themselves.

**3.** People use energy to grow and to move.

**4.** A cow eats plants that got energy from sunlight.

**5.** Sample answers: Fruits—apple, banana, blueberry, watermelon; Vegetables—broccoli, carrot, celery, lettuce

## Seeds On the Move, pages 15–16

**1.** Wind blows on the white fluff, pushing the seed far away from the dandelion plant.

**2.** Wind can blow the seed away from the maple tree.

**3.** People can plant seeds in different places. People can sell or give seeds to people in different places.

## Helping Each Other, pages 17–18

**1.** plants, animals

**2.** plants, people

**3.** plants, animals

**4.** people, plants

**5.** plants, people

**6.** animals, plants

**7.** animals, plants

## Growing Plants for Food, pages 19–20

**1.** Plants need space for their roots and to get enough light.

**2.** Vegetables can grow in greenhouses during winter.

**3.** It does not need time to travel or be bought.

**4.** Answers will vary. Encourage recognition of foods made mostly from plants, such as bread, spaghetti sauce, cereal, and soups.

## Plant Parts: I Ate That? page 21

cauliflower: flower; onions: bulb; lettuce: leaf; pear: fruit; melon: fruit; beet: root; peas: seeds; lemon: fruit; zucchini: fruit; corn: seeds; carrot: root; eggplant: fruit; asparagus: stem; apple: fruit

**Create a Board Game About Plants, page 22**
Have students play their board game with a partner.

**Plants Quiz, page 23**
1. stem, sepals, stamen
2. petal, pistil
3. sprout, seedling
4. manure
5. oxygen, orchard
6. water, warmth
7. flower, fruit
8. energy
9. greenhouse, garden

# Unit: Forces and Movement

**What Can Forces Do? pages 24–25**
1. pull
2. push
3. push
4. pull
5. Sparky pulled the leash to make Tanya run. Tanya pulled the leash to make Sparky slow down. Sparky pulled Tanya off the sidewalk and through the garden.
6. The change from walking to running (two times) and from running to slowing down.
7. Sparky pulls Tanya off the sidewalk and through Mr. Lee's flower garden.

**The Force of Gravity, pages 26–27**
1. Gravity pulls you toward the ground.
2. You move faster near the bottom of the slide. You can feel the change in speed.
3. Without gravity, juice would not fall from the container.
4. Gravity keeps the bicycle wheels on the ground so they can push against the ground.

**The Force of Magnets, pages 28–29**
1. pull together
2. push apart
3. pull together
4. push apart
5. Magnetic force can make an object stop moving. Magnetic force can change the direction of a moving object.

**The Force of Friction, pages 30–31**
1. The towel.
2. A towel has a rougher surface than a glass table. Rough surfaces create more friction than smooth surfaces do.
3. There is more friction when you rub together two pieces of

sandpaper. Sandpaper has a rougher surface than regular paper and it is harder to rub them together.
4. A paved road is smooth and creates little friction. Gravel adds a lot of bumps to the surface, giving the road more friction.

**How Friction Helps Us, pages 32–33**
1. Sock feet are more dangerous on stairs because they are smooth. The soles of shoes create more friction.
2. Snow tires, because they create more friction on icy roads.
3. The rougher surface on snow tires will slow cars down more. Regular tires slow cars down less. There is no need for snow tires when there is no snow and ice.

**A Snowy Day, pages 34–35**
1. gravity
2. muscular force
3. friction
4. magnetic force
5 and 6. Sample answer: Milk pours down onto Ryan's cereal; Snowflakes fall from the sky.
7 and 8. Sample answer: Mom lifts and tilts the milk container. Kim pulls the shopping list from under the magnet. Kim writes on the shopping list. Mom picks up Ryan. Mom pushes Ryan's cereal bowl.

**Contact and Non-contact Forces, pages 36–37**
1. Contact forces: friction, muscular force; Non-contact forces: magnetic force, gravity
2. No, non-contact forces still work when there is contact between objects. The magnetic force keeps the pin stuck to the magnet even after they are in contact. The rock does not float because the force of gravity is pulling on it, even when the rock is touching Earth.

**Experiment: The Force of Static Electricity, pages 38–39**
1. A pulling force, because it pulls the water closer to the comb.
2. Non-contact force, because the static electricity in the comb pulls on the water without touching it.
3. No, a magnet only pulls on iron or nickel.
**Try It!** Students may notice that some pieces of foil shift position, some pieces stand on end and some pieces jump to the comb and stick to it.

**Wind and Water, pages 40–41**
1. Sample answer: Leaves blowing off trees, trees bending, flags flapping, kites flying, hats blowing off heads, curtains moving, long grass or crops in fields moving, clouds moving across the sky.
2. A tornado can blow down walls and break windows in a house, which can hurt people inside. Basements are underground, so wind cannot blow down basement walls.

3. A basement could quickly become filled with water during a flash flood.

4. Very strong wind creates large waves and pushes them onto land. Large waves can bring enough water onto land to cause a flood.

**Mix and Match Forces Game, pages 42–43**

| Game Card | Matching Square on Game Board |
|---|---|
| A force that happens when two things rub together. | Friction |
| A safer place in a house during a tornado. | The basement |
| A storm with wind that moves in circles | Tornado |
| Something created by the pushing force of wind | A wave |
| Examples of muscular force | Pushes and pulls you create with your body |
| Gravity | The pulling force that comes from Earth |
| Magnets have two of these | Poles |
| Push apart | What the north poles on two magnets do to each other |
| These create friction so we do not slip. | Rough soles on shoes |
| They make things start moving, stop moving, change speed, or change direction. | Things forces can do |
| This force makes a ball fall to the ground when you throw it. | Gravity |
| Two contact forces | Friction and muscular force |
| Two non-contact forces | Gravity and magnetic force |
| What a magnet attracts | Objects made of the metals nickel or iron |
| You create this when you comb your hair. | Static electricity |

# Unit: Stability and Structures

## What Is a Structure? pages 44–45

1. Support a load.

2. Sample answers: Airplane — passengers and cargo; Backpack — textbooks and food; Shopping cart — groceries and small child

3. Load — person; Purpose — transportation and tricks

4. Yes, because it holds a load (the weight of materials it is made of), it has a size and a shape, and it has a purpose (to keep people and/or animals in or out of an area).

## Natural Structures, pages 46–47

**Brain Stretch** Sample answers: bird nests, ant hills, beaver dams, spider webs

1. Sample answers: birds, eggs, materials used to build the nest

2. circular, shaped like a bowl

3. Sample answers: twigs, grass, moss, string, feathers, mud

4. Sample answers: to catch insects for food, home for the spider

5. Sample answers: the spider, any insects caught on the web, the strands used to build the web

6. No, because it was built by a human.

## Strength and Stability, pages 48–49

1. No, because the top piece of wood is bending and might break.

2. Yes, the two blocks on the bottom are the same height, so the step will not rock back and forth when someone is on it.

3. Strengthen the platform with another or a thicker piece of wood.

4. So a person will not fall off and get hurt.

## Choosing Materials, pages 50–51

1. Glass is see-through and stops wind.

2. Durable — It can last more than 1,000 years; Strong — It can support other parts of the building for a very long time.

3. To be gentle to people's feet and bend to allow natural walking movement.

## Experiment: Make a Paper Bridge, pages 52–53

1. The paper folded like a fan was strongest. The many layers make it stronger.

2. Some students might simply make the bridges as in the experiment, but with both pieces of paper. Other students might use the second piece of paper to make a support such as a tent shape or an arch, that adds strength to the bridge that spans the gap between the two stacks of books.

## Experiment: Center of Gravity, pages 54–55

1. Ruler alone: center; Ruler with eraser: a little closer to the eraser.

2. No, it will be closer to the erasers.

3. The mark should be placed closer to the heavier stack.

## Center of Gravity in Structures, pages 56–57
1. Vase B, because the wide part of the vase (near the bottom) is heavier than the narrow part.
2. Vase A, because it has a higher center of gravity (the heaviest part is near the top).
3. The bookcase could tip over because most weight would be at the top.

## Tension and Compression, pages 58–59
1. Tension, because people are pulling.
2. It gets longer.
3. Compression, because the weight of the tabletop pushes down on the legs.
4. The wood is harder.

## Building a Roof, pages 60–61
1. snow
2. workers and tools
3. A tie hold the ends of the struts in place so the roof cannot collapse.
4. Compression, because it is a pushing force.

## Structures Word Search, pages 62–63
1. purpose
2. web
3. load
4. stable
5. durable
6. center, gravity
7. tie, strut
8. flexible
9. Tension

| B | E | V | G | A | I | S | P | D | Y | C | O |
|---|---|---|---|---|---|---|---|---|---|---|---|
| F | L | O | A | D | S | T | A | B | L | E | L |
| A | B | D | V | S | O | R | H | I | A | F | M |
| S | I | G | I | H | D | U | R | A | B | L | E |
| O | X | I | R | C | O | T | X | E | W | O | S |
| I | E | T | L | A | E | Y | B | I | E | G | O |
| M | L | A | O | Z | V | N | A | T | B | F | P |
| A | F | B | Y | O | G | I | T | S | A | E | R |
| T | E | N | S | I | O | N | T | E | Z | T | U |
| E | K | I | W | C | N | J | X | Y | R | U | P |

## Structures Collage, page 64
Create a bulletin board display of students' collages.

# Unit: Soil and the Environment

## Why Is Soil Important? pages 65–66
1. Sample answer: backyard; trees, grass, weeds, flowers, and bushes.
2. Fruits and vegetables grow in soil. Some animals that provide food, such as cows, need to eat plants that grow in soil.
3. Sample answers: pencils, rulers, desks, tables, paper, books, bookshelves
4. Wood comes from trees. Trees need soil to grow.
5. Sample answers: strawberries, apples, carrots, corn, peaches, bread, potatoes, peas, tomatoes, oranges, grapefruit, grapes, cucumbers, lettuce, raspberries, nuts

## What Is Soil Made Of? pages 67–68
1. Living Things: ants, roots, bacteria, worms; Nonliving Things: water, sand, air, pebbles, rock, salt, sticks, dead leaves
2. Air is found in the tiny spaces in soil.
3. Answers will vary.

## Soil Particles, pages 69–70
1. sugar, powdered drink mix, salt
2. touch
3. Smallest: clay; Medium: silt; Largest: sand
4. The cup with clay contains the most particles because clay particles are smallest, so more clay particles fit in the cup.
5. Rub each type of particle between your fingers and notice how each type feels.

## Air and Water in Soil, pages 71–72
1. The cup with large stones.
2. The water went into the spaces between the stones.
3. The air is in the spaces between the particles.
4. The cup with silt particles has the most air. There is more space for air between the silt particles because they are larger than clay particles.

## Experiment: What Is in This Soil? pages 73–74
1. Students may or may not notice bubbles.
2. Air rising from the spaces between the particles in the soil.
3. The soil was probably uniform to start then settled in layers.

**Air and Water for Plant Roots, pages 75–76**

1. Water pushes air out of the spaces between the particles so the roots do not have access to air.
2. The cup with stones has larger spaces between the particles.
3. Water will flow faster through the cup with stones because there are larger spaces between the particles.
4. The water would flow faster through Abdul's cup. Silt particles are larger than clay particles, so there are larger spaces between the silt particles.

**Nutrients in Soil, pages 77–78**

1. a piece of plastic bag, a bone his dog buried, a stone, a nail, a piece of broken glass
2. When it rains or when people water their gardens, the nutrients in the fertilizer mix with the water, and the water moves down through the soil to where the roots are.
3. Bacteria release the nutrients from dead plants and animals into the soil. Plants can take in the nutrients once they mix with water.
4. Grass clippings contain nutrients that grass needs to grow.

**Three Types of Soil, pages 79–80**

1. Clay soil because it drains very slowly and sticks together very well when squeezed.
2. The roots are not getting enough air.
3. Loam, because it drains faster and holds moisture.
4. The plant's roots need more water. Sandy soil drains quickly, so the roots do not have enough time to take in water.

**Wonderful Worms! pages 81–82**

1. The tunnels help the soil drain faster.
2. Plant roots grow into the spaces created by a worm tunnel.
3. Worms release the nutrients from dead things when they leave behind castings.

**How Nature Recycles, page 83**

1. Forest plants get water from rain and nutrients from dead things and animal waste (castings and manure).

**Composting, pages 84–85**

1. Sample answer: Composting is a good way to recycle leaves, and fruit and vegetable scraps. Over time, the waste decomposes and turns into rich soil called compost. Compost can be dug into flowerbeds, vegetable gardens, put on lawns, and under trees and bushes. Compost gives a boost of nutrients to the soil wherever it is used.

**George Washington Carver, pages 86–87**

1. George went to school as a child. Other child slaves worked hard on farms.
2. The farmers could not grow strong, healthy cotton plants because there were not enough nutrients in the soil.
3. Planting peas or peanuts helped cotton farmers because these plants put nutrients back into the soil. Cotton plants need the nutrients to grow strong and healthy.
4. George was called "the farmer's best friend" because he invented many new ways for people to use the plants farmers grew.
5. Americans celebrate January 5 as George Washington Carver Day.

**Soil Review, page 88**

1. Sample answer: worms, insects, bacteria
2. Sample answer: water, air, rocks, fertilizer, pesticide
3. clay, silt, sand
4. Plant roots take in nutrients that have mixed in water.
5. Loam is the best soil for most plants because it does not drain too quickly or too slowly.
6. Worm tunnels make paths for air in the soil, help water drain, and allow plants roots to more easily grow deeper into the soil.

**Early Engineers: The Wright Brothers, pages 90–91**

1. The most important event was that the Wright brothers made the first flight on record.
2. Sample answer: They read many books, loved to work on science projects, made a printing press, and opened a bicycle shop. These projects helped them become better designers.
3. They chose Kitty Hawk because it had sand dunes so they could land softly.
4. Sample answer: I think the Wright brothers were able to invent the first plane because they worked on lots of science projects and they had a bicycle shop. Because of that, they knew how things such as air, gears, and motors worked, and they used their knowledge to make a plane.
5. Answers will vary. Students might ask how they felt when their plane flew for the very first time.

**Early Engineers: Alexander Graham Bell, pages 92–93**

1. As a boy, Alexander loved doing experiments to learn new things.
2. Alexander's workshop was a place where he could dream up new inventions.
3. Alexander taught deaf children how to speak, and speaking is making sounds.
4. The speaker's voice was sent through a wire to the listener.

5. Answers will vary. Students might say the telephone helps people by allowing them to talk to people who are far away; letting them get in touch with police, fire, and ambulance services quickly; helping people keep in touch with friends and neighbors when they cannot or do not have time to visit them.

6. Alexander built and flew kites to learn how things fly.

### Early Inventions: Telephones from the Past, pages 94–96

1. The bottom part of the phone looks like a tall candle in a candleholder.
2. The part that people held in their hand is called the handset. The answer is in the labeled diagram of a rotary phone.
3. Sample answer: I would like to try using a rotary phone because it would be fun to use the dial.
4. Sample answer: A cell phone has a screen and a rotary phone does not.
5. Sample answer: The ability to take pictures and movies, make video calls, play games and music, use apps.

### New Inventions: The Clean Water Book, pages 97–98

1. Teri's invention makes water clean so people don't get sick from germs in the water.
2. The water that comes out of our taps is clean and does not have germs in it.
3. Sample answers: washing machine, dishwasher, coffeemaker, kettle, tap, hose, refrigerator that makes ice cubes, hose, lawn sprinkler, mop, humidifier

### Brain Stretch, page 98

Sample answers: taking showers or baths, washing clothes, washing dishes, cleaning floors, watering plants

### Amazing Robots, pages 99–101

1. The vacuum cleaners are robots because they do something that people can do. People can move a vacuum cleaner across a floor. This vacuum cleaner moves itself across a floor.
2. Answers will vary. Encourage students to explain how the structure of the robot is related to its function.

### Engineers Make Our Lives Better, page 104

Ask volunteers to share with the class what pictures they chose and why they chose them. Alternatively, create a bulletin board display of students' pictures.